HOLT SCIENCE & TECHNOLOGY

Microorganisms, Fungi, and Plants

HOLT, RINEHART AND WINSTON

A Harcourt Classroom Education Company

Austin • New York • Orlando • Atlanta • San Francisco • Boston • Dallas • Toronto • London

Acknowledgments

Chapter Writers

Katy Z. Allen
*Science Writer and Former
Biology Teacher*
Wayland, Massachusetts

Linda Ruth Berg, Ph.D.
*Adjunct Professor–Natural
Sciences*
St. Petersburg Junior College
St. Petersburg, Florida

Jennie Dusheck
Science Writer
Santa Cruz, California

Mark F. Taylor, Ph.D.
Associate Professor of Biology
Baylor University
Waco, Texas

Lab Writers

Diana Scheidle Bartos
Science Consultant and Educator
Diana Scheidle Bartos, L.L.C.
Lakewood, Colorado

Carl Benson
General Science Teacher
Plains High School
Plains, Montana

Charlotte Blassingame
Technology Coordinator
White Station Middle School
Memphis, Tennessee

Marsha Carver
Science Teacher and Dept. Chair
McLean County High School
Calhoun, Kentucky

Kenneth E. Creese
Science Teacher
White Mountain Junior High
School
Rock Springs, Wyoming

Linda Culp
Science Teacher and Dept. Chair
Thorndale High School
Thorndale, Texas

James Deaver
Science Teacher and Dept. Chair
West Point High School
West Point, Nebraska

Frank McKinney, Ph.D.
Professor of Geology
Appalachian State University
Boone, North Carolina

Alyson Mike
Science Teacher
East Valley Middle School
East Helena, Montana

C. Ford Morishita
Biology Teacher
Clackamas High School
Milwaukie, Oregon

Patricia D. Morrell, Ph.D.
*Assistant Professor, School of
Education*
University of Portland
Portland, Oregon

Hilary C. Olson, Ph.D.
Research Associate
Institute for Geophysics
The University of Texas
Austin, Texas

James B. Pulley
*Science Editor and Former
Science Teacher*
Liberty High School
Liberty, Missouri

Denice Lee Sandefur
Science Chairperson
Nucla High School
Nucla, Colorado

Patti Soderberg
Science Writer
The BioQUEST Curriculum
Consortium
Beloit College
Beloit, Wisconsin

Phillip Vavala
Science Teacher and Dept. Chair
Salesianum School
Wilmington, Delaware

Albert C. Wartski
Biology Teacher
Chapel Hill High School
Chapel Hill, North Carolina

Lynn Marie Wartski
*Science Writer and Former
Science Teacher*
Hillsborough, North Carolina

Ivora D. Washington
Science Teacher and Dept. Chair
Hyattsville Middle School
Washington, D.C.

Academic Reviewers

Renato J. Aguilera, Ph.D.
Associate Professor
Department of Molecular, Cell,
and Developmental Biology
University of California
Los Angeles, California

David M. Armstrong, Ph.D.
Professor of Biology
Department of E.P.O. Biology
University of Colorado
Boulder, Colorado

Alissa Arp, Ph.D.
*Director and Professor of
Environmental Studies*
Romberg Tiburon Center
San Francisco State University
Tiburon, California

Russell M. Brengelman
Professor of Physics
Morehead State University
Morehead, Kentucky

John A. Brockhaus, Ph.D.
*Director of Mapping, Charting,
and Geodesy Program*
Department of Geography and
Environmental Engineering
United States Military Academy
West Point, New York

Linda K. Butler, Ph.D.
Lecturer of Biological Sciences
The University of Texas
Austin, Texas

Barry Chernoff, Ph.D.
Associate Curator
Division of Fishes
The Field Museum of Natural
History
Chicago, Illinois

**Donna Greenwood
Crenshaw, Ph.D.**
Instructor
Department of Biology
Duke University
Durham, North Carolina

Hugh Crenshaw, Ph.D.
Assistant Professor of Zoology
Duke University
Durham, North Carolina

Joe W. Crim, Ph.D.
Professor of Biology
University of Georgia
Athens, Georgia

Peter Demmin, Ed.D.
*Former Science Teacher and
Chair*
Amherst Central High School
Amherst, New York

Joseph L. Graves, Jr., Ph.D.
*Associate Professor of
Evolutionary Biology*
Arizona State University West
Phoenix, Arizona

William B. Guggino, Ph.D.
*Professor of Physiology and
Pediatrics*
The Johns Hopkins University
School of Medicine
Baltimore, Maryland

David Haig, Ph.D.
Assistant Professor of Biology
Department of Organismic
and Evolutionary Biology
Harvard University
Cambridge, Massachusetts

Roy W. Hann, Jr., Ph.D.
Professor of Civil Engineering
Texas A&M University
College Station, Texas

Acknowledgments (cont.)

John E. Hoover, Ph.D.
Associate Professor of Biology
Millersville University
Millersville, Pennsylvania

Joan E. N. Hudson, Ph.D.
Associate Professor of Biological Sciences
Sam Houston State University
Huntsville, Texas

Laurie Jackson-Grusby, Ph.D.
Research Scientist and Doctoral Associate
Whitehead Institute for Biomedical Research
Massachusetts Institute of Technology
Cambridge, Massachusetts

George M. Langford, Ph.D.
Professor of Biological Sciences
Dartmouth College
Hanover, New Hampshire

Melanie C. Lewis, Ph.D.
Professor of Biology, Retired
Southwest Texas State University
San Marcos, Texas

V. Patteson Lombardi, Ph.D.
Research Assistant Professor of Biology
Department of Biology
University of Oregon
Eugene, Oregon

Glen Longley, Ph.D.
Professor of Biology and Director of the Edwards Aquifer Research Center
Southwest Texas State University
San Marcos, Texas

William F. McComas, Ph.D.
Director of the Center to Advance Science Education
University of Southern California
Los Angeles, California

LaMoine L. Motz, Ph.D.
Coordinator of Science Education
Oakland County Schools
Waterford, Michigan

Nancy Parker, Ph.D.
Associate Professor of Biology
Southern Illinois University
Edwardsville, Illinois

Barron S. Rector, Ph.D.
Associate Professor and Extension Range Specialist
Texas Agricultural Extension Service
Texas A&M University
College Station, Texas

Peter Sheridan, Ph.D.
Professor of Chemistry
Colgate University
Hamilton, New York

Miles R. Silman, Ph.D.
Assistant Professor of Biology
Wake Forest University
Winston-Salem, North Carolina

Neil Simister, Ph.D.
Associate Professor of Biology
Department of Life Sciences
Brandeis University
Waltham, Massachusetts

Lee Smith, Ph.D.
Curriculum Writer
MDL Information Systems, Inc.
San Leandro, California

Robert G. Steen, Ph.D.
Manager, Rat Genome Project
Whitehead Institute—Center for Genome Research
Massachusetts Institute of Technology
Cambridge, Massachusetts

Martin VanDyke, Ph.D.
Professor of Chemistry Emeritus
Front Range Community College
Westminister, Colorado

E. Peter Volpe, Ph.D.
Professor of Medical Genetics
Mercer University School of Medicine
Macon, Georgia

Harold K. Voris, Ph.D.
Curator and Head
Division of Amphibians and Reptiles
The Field Museum of Natural History
Chicago, Illinois

Mollie Walton
Biology Instructor
El Paso Community College
El Paso, Texas

Peter Wetherwax, Ph.D.
Professor of Biology
University of Oregon
Eugene, Oregon

Mary K. Wicksten, Ph.D.
Professor of Biology
Texas A&M University
College Station, Texas

R. Stimson Wilcox, Ph.D.
Associate Professor of Biology
Department of Biological Sciences
Binghamton University
Binghamton, New York

Conrad M. Zapanta, Ph.D.
Research Engineer
Sulzer Carbomedics, Inc.
Austin, Texas

Safety Reviewer

Jack Gerlovich, Ph.D.
Associate Professor
School of Education
Drake University
Des Moines, Iowa

Teacher Reviewers

Barry L. Bishop
Science Teacher and Dept. Chair
San Rafael Junior High School
Ferron, Utah

Carol A. Bornhorst
Science Teacher and Dept. Chair
Bonita Vista Middle School
Chula Vista, California

Paul Boyle
Science Teacher
Perry Heights Middle School
Evansville, Indiana

Yvonne Brannum
Science Teacher and Dept. Chair
Hine Junior High School
Washington, D.C.

Gladys Cherniak
Science Teacher
St. Paul's Episcopal School
Mobile, Alabama

James Chin
Science Teacher
Frank A. Day Middle School
Newtonville, Massachusetts

Kenneth Creese
Science Teacher
White Mountain Junior High School
Rock Springs, Wyoming

Linda A. Culp
Science Teacher and Dept. Chair
Thorndale High School
Thorndale, Texas

Georgiann Delgadillo
Science Teacher
East Valley Continuous Curriculum School
Spokane, Washington

Alonda Droege
Biology Teacher
Evergreen High School
Seattle, Washington

Michael J. DuPré
Curriculum Specialist
Rush Henrietta Junior-Senior High School
Henrietta, New York

Rebecca Ferguson
Science Teacher
North Ridge Middle School
North Richland Hills, Texas

Susan Gorman
Science Teacher
North Ridge Middle School
North Richland Hills, Texas

Gary Habeeb
Science Mentor
Sierra-Plumas Joint Unified School District
Downieville, California

Karma Houston-Hughes
Science Mentor
Kyrene Middle School
Tempe, Arizona

Roberta Jacobowitz
Science Teacher
C. W. Otto Middle School
Lansing, Michigan

Kerry A. Johnson
Science Teacher
Isbell Middle School
Santa Paula, California

M. R. Penny Kisiah
Science Teacher and Dept. Chair
Fairview Middle School
Tallahassee, Florida

Kathy LaRoe
Science Teacher
East Valley Middle School
East Helena, Montana

Jane M. Lemons
Science Teacher
Western Rockingham Middle School
Madison, North Carolina

Scott Mandel, Ph.D.
Director and Educational Consultant
Teachers Helping Teachers
Los Angeles, California

Thomas Manerchia
Former Biology and Life Science Teacher
Archmere Academy
Claymont, Delaware

Maurine O. Marchani
Science Teacher and Dept. Chair
Raymond Park Middle School
Indianapolis, Indiana

Jason P. Marsh
Biology Teacher
Montevideo High School and Montevideo Country School
Montevideo, Minnesota

Edith C. McAlanis
Science Teacher and Dept. Chair
Socorro Middle School
El Paso, Texas

Kevin McCurdy, Ph.D.
Science Teacher
Elmwood Junior High School
Rogers, Arkansas

Kathy McKee
Science Teacher
Hoyt Middle School
Des Moines, Iowa

Acknowledgments continue on page 167.

A Microorganisms, Fungi, and Plants

CHAPTER 1 It's Alive!! Or, Is It? 2
  1 Characteristics of Living Things 4
  2 The Simple Bare Necessities of Life 8
  3 The Chemistry of Life 10

CHAPTER 2 Bacteria and Viruses 22
  1 Bacteria 24
  2 Bacteria's Role in the World 29
  3 Viruses 33

CHAPTER 3 Protists and Fungi 44
  1 Protists 46
  2 Fungi 57

CHAPTER 4 Introduction to Plants 72
  1 What Makes a Plant a Plant? 74
  2 Seedless Plants 78
  3 Plants with Seeds 82
  4 The Structures of Seed Plants 88

CHAPTER 5 Plant Processes 104
  1 The Reproduction of Flowering Plants . . 106
  2 The Ins and Outs of Making Food 110
  3 Plant Responses to the Environment . . 113

Skills Development

Process Skills

QuickLabs

Starch Search 11
Spying on Spirilla 26
Moldy Bread 59
Observe a Mushroom 61
Moss Mass 79
Thirsty Seeds 108
Which Way Is Up? 114

Chapter Labs

Roly-Poly Races 14
Viral Decorations 36
There's a Fungus Among Us! 64
Leaf Me Alone! 96
Food Factory Waste 118

Skills Development *(continued)*

Research and Critical Thinking Skills

Apply

Are Computers Alive? 7

Ingenious Engineering! 31

A Mushroom Omelet 61

The Accidental Garden 83

Can Trees Tell Time? 116

Feature Articles

Scientific Debate

• Life on Mars? 20

Science Fiction

• "They're Made Out of Meat" 21

Science, Technology, and Society

• Edible Vaccines 42

• Moldy Bandages 70

• Supersquash or Frankenfruit? 102

Health Watch

• Helpful Viruses 43

Across the Sciences

• It's Alive! 71

Careers

• Ethnobotanist 103

Weird Science

• Mutant Mustard 124

Eye on the Environment

• A Rainbow of Cotton 125

Connections

Oceanography Connection

- Antifreeze Fish 5

Chemistry Connection

- Crystal Viruses 34
- Glowing Protists 50

Geology Connection

- Rocky Remains 53

Environment Connection

- Animals and Seeds 83

Astronomy Connection

- Seasons and the Sun 115

Mathematics

- How Much Oxygen 11
- Airborne Organisms 24
- Sizing Up a Virus 33
- Multiplying Yeasts 60
- Practice with Percents 77
- Bending by Degrees 113

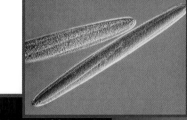

LabBook 126

Appendix 140

Concept Mapping 140

SI Measurement 141

Temperature Scales 142

Measuring Skills 143

Scientific Method 144

Making Charts and Graphs 147

Math Refresher 150

Periodic Table of the Elements 154

The Six Kingdoms 156

Using the Microscope 158

Glossary 160

Index 163

Self-Check Answers 168

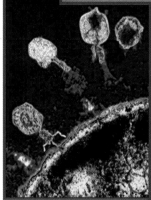

To the Student

This book was created to make your science experience interesting, exciting, and fun!

Go for It!

Science is a process of discovery, a trek into the unknown. The skills you develop using *Holt Science & Technology*— such as observing, experimenting, and explaining observations and ideas— are the skills you will need for the future. There is a universe of exploration and discovery awaiting those who accept the challenges of science.

Science & Technology

You see the interaction between science and technology every day. Science makes technology possible. On the other hand, some of the products of technology, such as computers, are used to make further scientific discoveries. In fact, much of the scientific work that is done today has become so technically complicated and expensive that no one person can do it entirely alone. But make no mistake, the creative ideas for even the most highly technical and expensive scientific work still come from individuals.

Activities and Labs

The activities and labs in this book will allow you to make some basic but important scientific discoveries on your own. You can even do some exploring on your own at home! Here's your chance to use your imagination and curiosity as you investigate your world.

Keep a ScienceLog

In this book, you will be asked to keep a type of journal called a ScienceLog to record your thoughts, observations, experiments, and conclusions. As you develop your ScienceLog, you will see your own ideas taking shape over time. You'll have a written record of how your ideas have changed as you learn about and explore interesting topics in science.

Know "What You'll Do"

The "What You'll Do" list at the beginning of each section is your built-in guide to what you need to learn in each chapter. When you can answer the questions in the Section Review and Chapter Review, you know you are ready for a test.

Check Out the Internet

You will see this $^{SCi}_{LINKS}$ logo throughout the book. You'll be using *sci*LINKS as your gateway to the Internet. Once you log on to *sci*LINKS using your computer's Internet link, type in the *sci*LINKS address. When asked for the keyword code, type in the keyword for that topic. A wealth of resources is now at your disposal to help you learn more about that topic.

In addition to *sci*LINKS you can log on to some other great resources to go with your text. The addresses shown below will take you to the home page of each site.

 internet**connect**

This textbook contains the following on-line resources to help you make the most of your science experience.

go. hrw .com

Visit **go.hrw.com** for extra help and study aids matched to your textbook. Just type in the keyword HST HOME.

Visit **www.scilinks.org** to find resources specific to topics in your textbook. Keywords appear throughout your book to take you further.

 Smithsonian Institution®
Internet Connections

Visit **www.si.edu/hrw** for specifically chosen on-line materials from one of our nation's premier science museums.

CNNfyi.com

Visit **www.cnnfyi.com** for late-breaking news and current events stories selected just for you.

It's Alive!! Or, Is It?

Sections

(1) Characteristics of
Living Things 4
Oceanography
Connection 5
Apply 7
Internet Connect 7

(2) The Simple Bare Necessities
of Life 8
Internet Connect 9

(3) The Chemistry of Life. . . . 10
MathBreak 11
QuickLab 11

Chapter Lab 14

Chapter Review 18

Feature Articles 20, 21

LabBook 130–135

Pre-Reading Questions

1. What characteristics do all living things have in common?
2. What do organisms need in order to stay alive?

ROBOT BUGS!

What does it mean to say something is *alive*? Machines have some of the characteristics of living things, but they do not have all of them. This amazing robot insect can respond to changes in its environment. It can walk over obstacles. It can perform some tasks. But it is still not alive. How is it like and unlike the living insect pictured here? In this chapter, you'll learn about the characteristics that all living things share.

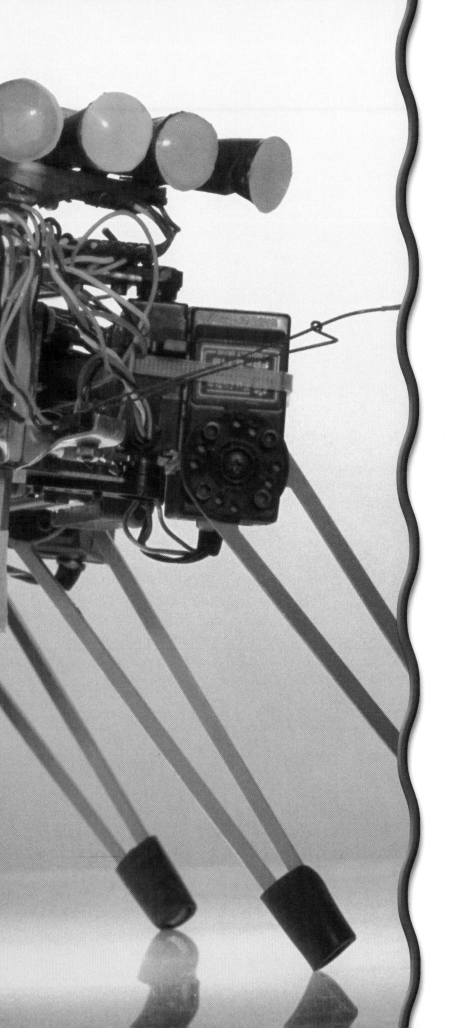

Activity

LIGHTS ON!

Living things respond to change. In this activity, you will work with a partner to see how eyes react to changes in light.

Procedure

1. Observe a classmate's eyes in a room with normal light. Find the pupil, which is the black area in the center of the colored part of the eye, and note its size.

2. Have your partner keep both eyes open, and have him or her cover each one with a cupped hand. Wait about 1 minute.

3. Instruct your partner to pull away both hands quickly. Immediately look at your partner's pupils. Record what happens.

4. Now briefly shine a **flashlight** into your partner's eyes. In your ScienceLog, record how this affects the pupils.

   Caution: Do not use the sun as the source of the light.

5. Change places with your partner, and repeat steps 1–4 so that your partner can observe your eyes.

Analysis

6. How did your partner's eyes respond to changes in the level of light?

7. How did changes in the size of your pupils affect your vision? What does this tell you about why pupils change size?

It's Alive!! Or, Is It?   **3**

Characteristics of Living Things

Terms to Learn

cell
stimulus
homeostasis
asexual
  reproduction

sexual
  reproduction
DNA
heredity
metabolism

What You'll Do

- List the characteristics of living things.
- Distinguish between asexual reproduction and sexual reproduction.
- Define and describe homeostasis.

While out in your yard one day, you notice something strange in the grass. It's slimy, bright yellow, and about the size of a dime. You have no idea what it is. Is it a plant part that fell from a tree? Is it alive? How can you tell?

Even though an amazing variety of living things exist on Earth, they are all alike in several ways. What does a dog have in common with a tree? What does a fish have in common with a mushroom? And what do *you* have in common with a slimy blob (also known as a slime mold)? Read on to find out about the six characteristics that all organisms share.

Slime mold

1 Living Things Have Cells

Every living thing is composed of one or more cells. A **cell** is a membrane-covered structure that contains all of the materials necessary for life. The membrane that surrounds a cell separates the contents of the cell from the cell's environment.

Many organisms, such as those in **Figure 1,** are made up of only one cell. Other organisms, such as the monkeys and trees in **Figure 2,** are made up of trillions of cells. Most cells are too small to be seen with the naked eye.

In an organism with many cells, cells perform specialized functions. For example, your nerve cells are specialized to transport signals, and your muscle cells are specialized for movement.

Figure 1 *Each of these organisms is made of only one cell.*

Figure 2 *Trillions of cells make up these organisms.*

2 Living Things Sense and Respond to Change

All organisms have the ability to sense change in their environment and to respond to that change. When your pupils are exposed to light, they respond by becoming smaller. A change in an organism's environment that affects the activity of the organism is called a **stimulus** (plural, *stimuli*).

Stimuli can be chemicals, gravity, darkness, light, sounds, tastes, or anything that causes organisms to respond in some way. A gentle touch causes a response in the plant shown in **Figure 3**.

✓ **Self-Check**

Is your alarm clock a stimulus? Explain. *(See page 168 to check your answer.)*

Figure 3 *The touch of an insect triggers the Venus' flytrap to quickly close its leaves.*

Homeostasis Even though an organism's external environment may change, the organism must maintain a stable internal environment to survive. This is because the life processes of organisms involve many different kinds of chemical reactions that can occur only in delicately balanced environments. The maintenance of a stable internal environment is called **homeostasis** (HOH mee OH STAY sis).

Your body maintains a temperature of about 37°C. When you get hot, your body responds by sweating. When you get cold, your muscles twitch in an attempt to generate heat. This causes you to shiver. Whether you are sweating or shivering, your body is trying to return things to normal. Another example of homeostasis is your body's ability to maintain a stable amount of sugar in your blood.

Oceanography
C O N N E C T I O N

Fish that live in the ice-cold waters off Antarctica make a natural antifreeze that keeps them from freezing.

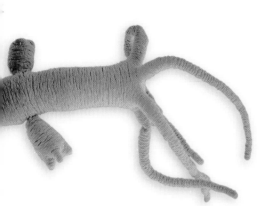

3 Living Things Reproduce

Organisms make other organisms like themselves. This is accomplished in one of two ways: by asexual reproduction or by sexual reproduction. In **asexual reproduction,** a single parent produces offspring that are identical to the parent. **Figure 4** shows an organism that reproduces asexually. Most single-celled organisms reproduce in this way. **Sexual reproduction,** however, almost always requires two parents to produce offspring that will share characteristics of both parents. Most animals and plants reproduce in this way. The bear cubs in **Figure 5** were produced sexually by their parents.

Figure 4 *The hydra can reproduce asexually by forming buds that will break off and grow into new individuals.*

Figure 5 *Like most animals, bears produce offspring by sexual reproduction.*

4 Living Things Have DNA

The cells of all living things contain a special molecule called **DNA** (**d**eoxyribo**n**ucleic **a**cid). DNA provides instructions for making molecules called *proteins*. Proteins take part in almost all of the activities of an organism's cells. Proteins also determine many of an organism's characteristics.

When organisms reproduce, they pass on copies of their DNA to their offspring. The transmission of characteristics from one generation to the next is called **heredity.** Offspring, such as the children in **Figure 6,** resemble their parents because of heredity.

Figure 6 *Children resemble their parents because of heredity.*

5 Living Things Use Energy

Organisms use energy to carry out the activities of life. These activities include such things as making food, breaking down food, moving materials into and out of cells, and building cells. An organism's **metabolism** (muh TAB uh LIZ uhm) is the total of all of the chemical activities that it performs.

Are Computers Alive?
Computers can do all kinds of things, such as storing information and doing complex calculations. Some computers have even been programmed to learn, that is, to get better and faster at solving problems over time. Do you think computers could become so advanced that they should be considered alive? Why or why not?

6 Living Things Grow and Develop

All living things, whether they are made of one cell or many cells, grow during periods of their lives. Growth in single-celled organisms occurs as the cell gets larger. Organisms made of many cells grow mainly by increasing their number of cells.

In addition to getting larger, living things may develop and change as they grow. Just like the organisms in **Figure 7,** you will pass through different stages in your life as you develop into an adult.

Figure 7 Over time, acorns develop into oak seedlings, which become oak trees.

SECTION REVIEW

1. What characteristics of living things does a river have? Is a river alive?

2. What does the fur coat of a bear have to do with homeostasis?

3. How is reproduction related to heredity?

4. **Applying Concepts** What are some stimuli in your environment? How do you respond to these stimuli?

internet connect

SCi*LINKS*
NSTA

TOPIC: Characteristics of Living Things
GO TO: www.scilinks.org
*sci***LINKS NUMBER:** HSTL030

Terms to Learn

producer
consumer
decomposer

What You'll Do

◆ Explain why organisms need food, water, air, and living space.
◆ Discuss how living things obtain what they need to live.

The Simple Bare Necessities of Life

Would it surprise you to learn that you have the same basic needs as a tree, a frog, or a fly? In fact, almost every organism has the same basic needs: food, water, air, and living space.

Food

All living things need food. Food provides organisms with the energy and raw materials needed to carry on life processes and to build and repair cells and body parts. But not all organisms get food in the same way. In fact, organisms can be grouped into three different categories based on how they get their food.

Making Food Some organisms, such as plants, are called **producers** because they can produce their own food. Like most producers, plants use energy from the sun to make food from water and carbon dioxide. Some producers obtain energy and food from the chemicals in their environment.

Getting Food Other organisms are called **consumers** because they must eat (consume) other organisms to get food. The salamander in **Figure 8** is an example of a consumer. It gets the energy it needs by eating insects and other organisms.

Some consumers are decomposers. **Decomposers** are organisms that get their food by breaking down the nutrients in dead organisms or animal wastes.

Figure 8 *The salamander is a consumer. The fungus is a decomposer, and the plants are producers.*

Water

You may have heard that your body is made mostly of water. In fact, your cells and the cells of almost all living organisms are approximately 70 percent water—even the cells of a cactus and a camel. Most of the chemical reactions involved in metabolism require water.

Organisms differ greatly in terms of how much water they need and how they obtain it. You could survive for only about 3 days without water. You obtain water from the fluids you drink and the food you eat. The desert-dwelling kangaroo rat never drinks. It gets all of its water from its food.

Air

Air is a mixture of several different gases, including oxygen and carbon dioxide. Animals, plants, and most other living things use oxygen in the chemical process that releases energy from food. Organisms that live on land get oxygen from the air. Organisms living in fresh water and salt water either take in dissolved oxygen from the water or come to the water's surface to get oxygen from the air. Some organisms, such as the European diving spider in **Figure 9,** go to great lengths to get oxygen.

Green plants, algae, and some bacteria need carbon dioxide gas in addition to oxygen. The food these organisms produce is made from carbon dioxide and water by *photosynthesis* (FOHT oh SIN thuh sis), the process that converts the energy in sunlight to energy stored in food.

Figure 9 *This spider surrounds itself with an air bubble so that it can obtain oxygen underwater.*

A Place to Live

All organisms must have somewhere to live that contains all of the things they need to survive. Some organisms, such as elephants, require a large amount of space. Other organisms, such as bacteria, may live their entire life in a single pore on the tip of your nose.

Because the amount of space on Earth is limited, organisms often compete with each other for food, water, and other necessities. Many animals, including the warbler in **Figure 10,** will claim a particular space and try to keep other animals away. Plants also compete with each other for living space and for access to water and sunlight.

Figure 10 *A warbler's song is more than just a pretty tune. The warbler is protecting its home by telling other warblers to stay out of its territory.*

SECTION REVIEW

1. Why are decomposers categorized as consumers? How do they differ from producers?

2. Why are most cells 70 percent water?

3. **Making Inferences** Could life as we know it exist on Earth if air contained only oxygen? Explain.

4. **Identifying Relationships** How might a cave, an ant, and a lake meet the needs of an organism?

Terms to Learn

protein   phospholipid
carbohydrate   nucleic acid
lipid   ATP

What You'll Do

◆ Compare and contrast the
  chemical building blocks of cells.
◆ Explain the importance of ATP.

The Chemistry of Life

All living things are made of cells, but what are cells made of? Everything, whether it is living or not, is made up of tiny building blocks called *atoms*. There are about 100 different kinds of atoms.

A substance made up of one type of atom is called an *element*. When two or more atoms join together, they form what's called a *molecule*. Molecules found in living things are usually made of different combinations of six elements: carbon, hydrogen, nitrogen, oxygen, phosphorous, and sulfur. These elements combine to form proteins, carbohydrates, lipids, nucleic acids, and ATP.

Proteins

Almost all of the life processes of a cell involve proteins. After water, proteins are the most abundant materials in cells. **Proteins** are large molecules that are made up of subunits called *amino acids*.

Organisms break down the proteins in food to supply their cells with amino acids. These amino acids are then linked together to form new proteins. Some proteins are made up of only a few amino acids, while others contain more than 10,000 amino acids.

Proteins in Action Proteins have many different functions. Some proteins form structures that are easy to see, such as those in **Figure 11.** Other proteins are at work at the cellular level. The protein *hemoglobin* (HEE moh GLOH bin) in red blood cells attaches to oxygen so that oxygen can be delivered throughout the body. Some proteins help protect cells from foreign materials. And special proteins called *enzymes* make many different chemical reactions in a cell occur quickly.

Figure 11 *Feathers, spider webs, and hair are all made of proteins.*

Carbohydrates

Carbohydrates are a group of compounds made of sugars. Cells use carbohydrates as a source of energy and for energy storage. When an organism needs energy, its cells break down carbohydrates to release the energy stored in the carbohydrates.

There are two types of carbohydrates, simple carbohydrates and complex carbohydrates. Simple carbohydrates are made of one sugar molecule or a few sugar molecules linked together. Table sugar and the sugar in fruits are examples of simple carbohydrates.

Too Much Sugar! When an organism has more sugar than it needs, its extra sugar may be stored in the form of complex carbohydrates. Complex carbohydrates are made of hundreds of sugar molecules linked together. Your body makes some complex carbohydrates and stores them in your liver. Plants make a complex carbohydrate called *starch*. A potato plant, such as the one in **Figure 12,** stores its extra sugar as starch. When you eat mashed potatoes or French fries, you are eating a potato plant's stored starch. Your body can then break down this complex carbohydrate to release the energy stored in it.

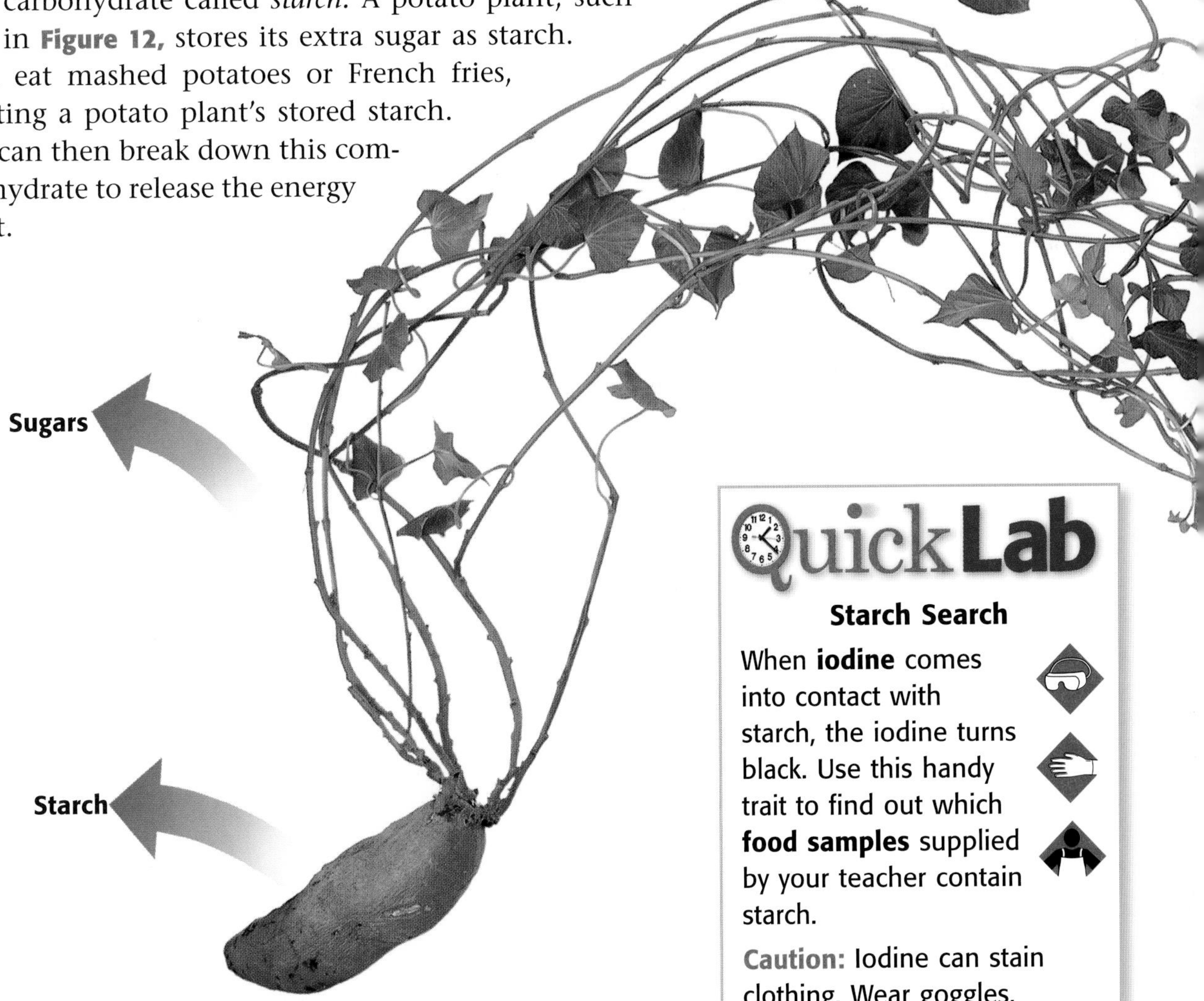

Sugars

Starch

Figure 12 *Most sugars are simple carbohydrates. The extra sugar in a potato plant is stored in the potato as starch, a complex carbohydrate.*

QuickLab

Starch Search

When **iodine** comes into contact with starch, the iodine turns black. Use this handy trait to find out which **food samples** supplied by your teacher contain starch.

Caution: Iodine can stain clothing. Wear goggles, protective gloves, and an apron.

Lipids

Lipids are compounds that cannot mix with water. Lipids have many important functions in the cell. Like carbohydrates, some lipids store energy. Other lipids form the membranes of cells.

Fats and Oils Fats and oils are lipids that store energy. When an organism has used up most of its carbohydrates, it can obtain energy from these lipids. The structures of fats and oils are almost identical, but at room temperature most fats are solid and oils are liquid. Most of the lipids stored in plants are oils, while most of the lipids stored in animals are fats.

Phospholipids All cells are surrounded by a structure called a *cell membrane*. **Phospholipids** are the molecules that form much of the cell membrane. As you read earlier, water is the most abundant material in a cell. When phospholipids are in water, the tails come together and the heads face out into the water. This happens because the head of a phospholipid molecule is attracted to water, while the tail is not. **Figure 13** shows how phospholipid molecules form two layers when they are in water.

Yeast cells get energy the same way other cells do. See for yourself on page 134 of the LabBook.

Figure 13 *The contents of a cell are surrounded by a membrane of phospholipid molecules.*

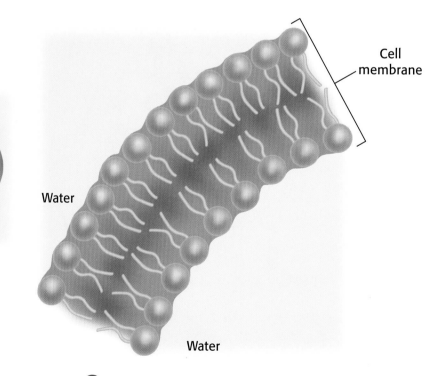

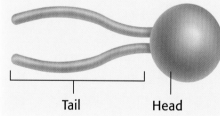

Phospholipid molecule

Tail   Head

a *The head of a phospholipid molecule is attracted to water, but the tail is not.*

b *When phospholipid molecules come together in water, they form two layers.*

Nucleic Acids

Nucleic acids are compounds made up of subunits called *nucleotides.* A nucleic acid may contain thousands of nucleotides. Nucleic acids are sometimes called the blueprints of life because they contain all the information needed for the cell to make all of its proteins.

DNA is a nucleic acid. A DNA molecule is like a recipe book titled *How to Make Proteins.* When a cell needs to make a certain protein, it gets information from DNA to direct how amino acids are hooked together to make that protein. You will learn more about DNA later.

The Cell's Fuel

Another molecule that is important to cells is ATP (**a**denosine **trip**hosphate). **ATP** is the major fuel used for all cell activities that require energy.

When food molecules, such as carbohydrates and fats, are broken down, some of the released energy is transferred to ATP molecules, as shown in **Figure 14.** The energy in carbohydrates and lipids must be transferred to ATP before the stored energy can be used by cells to fuel their life processes.

SECTION REVIEW

1. What are the subunits of proteins? of starch? of DNA?

2. What do carbohydrates, fats, and oils have in common?

3. Are all proteins enzymes? Explain your answer.

4. **Making Predictions** What would happen to the supply of ATP in your cells if you did not eat enough carbohydrates? How would this affect your cells?

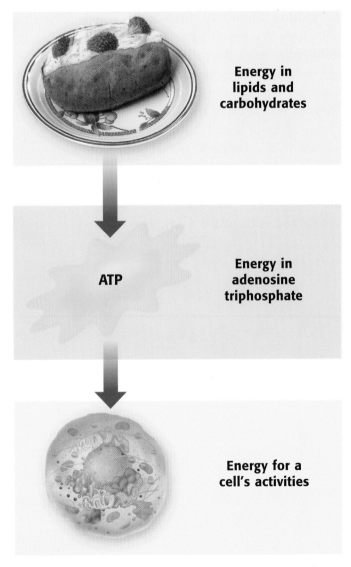

Energy in lipids and carbohydrates

ATP

Energy in adenosine triphosphate

Energy for a cell's activities

Figure 14 *The energy in the carbohydrates and lipids in food must be transferred to ATP molecules before cells can use the energy.*

Discovery Lab

Roly-Poly Races

Have you ever watched a bug run? Did you wonder why it was running? The bug you saw running was probably reacting to a stimulus. In other words, something happened that made it run! One characteristic of living things is that they respond to stimuli. In this activity, you will study the movement of roly-polies. Roly-polies are also called pill bugs. They are not really bugs at all. They are land-dwelling crustaceans called isopods. Isopods live in dark, moist places, often under rocks or wood. You will provide stimuli to determine how fast your isopod can move and what affects its speed and direction. Remember that isopods are living things and must be treated gently and with respect.

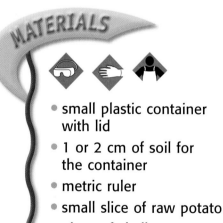

MATERIALS

- small plastic container with lid
- 1 or 2 cm of soil for the container
- metric ruler
- small slice of raw potato
- piece of chalk
- 4 isopods
- watch or clock with a second hand

Procedure

1. Choose a partner and decide together how you will organize your roly-poly race. Discuss some gentle ways you might be able to stimulate your isopods to move. Choose five or six things that might cause movement, such as a gentle nudge or a change in temperature, sound, or light. Check your choices with your teacher.

2. In your ScienceLog or on a computer, make a data table similar to the one below. Label your columns with the stimuli you've chosen. Label the rows "Isopod 1," "Isopod 2," "Isopod 3," and "Isopod 4."

Isopod Responses			
	Stimulus 1: ?	Stimulus 2: ?	Stimulus 3: ?
Isopod 1			
Isopod 2			
Isopod 3			
Isopod 4			

3 Place 1 or 2 cm of soil in a small plastic container. Add a small slice of potato and a piece of chalk. Your isopods will eat these things.

4 Place four isopods in your container. Observe them for a minute or two before you perform your tests. Record your observations in your ScienceLog.

5 Decide which stimulus you want to test first. Carefully arrange the isopods at the "starting line." The starting line can be an imaginary line at one end of the container.

6 Gently stimulate each isopod at the same time and in the same way. In your data table, record the isopods' responses to the stimulus. Be sure to measure and record the distance each isopod traveled. Don't forget to time the race.

7 Repeat steps 5–6 for each stimulus. Be sure to wait at least 2 minutes between trials.

Analysis

8 Describe the way isopods move. Do their legs move together?

9 Did your isopods move before or between the trials? Did the movement seem to have a purpose, or were the isopods responding to a stimulus? Explain your answer.

10 Did any of the stimuli you chose make the isopods move faster or go farther? Explain your answer.

Going Further
Isopods may not run for the joy of running like humans do. But humans, like all living things, react to stimuli. Describe three stimuli that might cause humans to run.

Chapter Highlights

SECTION 1

Vocabulary

cell *(p. 4)*

stimulus *(p. 5)*

homeostasis *(p. 5)*

asexual reproduction *(p. 6)*

sexual reproduction *(p. 6)*

DNA *(p. 6)*

heredity *(p. 6)*

metabolism *(p. 6)*

Section Notes

- All living things share the six characteristics of life.

- Organisms are made of one or more cells.

- Organisms detect and respond to stimuli in their environment.

- Organisms work to keep their internal environment stable so that the chemical activities of their cells are not disrupted. The maintenance of a stable internal environment is called homeostasis.

- Organisms reproduce and make more organisms like themselves. Offspring can be produced asexually or sexually.

- Offspring resemble their parents. The passing of characteristics from parent to offspring is called heredity.

- Organisms grow and may change during their lifetime.

- Organisms use energy to carry out the chemical activities of life. Metabolism is the sum of an organism's chemical activities.

SECTION 2

Vocabulary

producer *(p. 8)*

consumer *(p. 8)*

decomposer *(p. 8)*

Section Notes

- Organisms must have food. Producers make their own food. Consumers eat other organisms for food. Decomposers break down the nutrients in dead organisms and animal wastes.

☑ Skills Check

Math Concepts

HOW MANY? In the MathBreak on page 11, you determined how many molecules of oxygen a single red blood cell could carry.

$$\frac{250{,}000{,}000 \text{ molecules of hemoglobin}}{1 \text{ red blood cell}} \times \frac{4 \text{ molecules of oxygen}}{1 \text{ molecule of hemoglobin}}$$

$$= 1{,}000{,}000{,}000 \text{ molecules of oxygen}$$

Visual Understanding

PHOSPHOLIPIDS Look at the illustrations of phospholipids and the cell membrane on page 12. Notice that the fluid inside and outside of the cell contains a lot of water. The head of the phospholipid molecule is attracted to water. Therefore, the phospholipid molecules that form the cell membrane line up with their tails facing away from the water.

SECTION 2

- Organisms depend on water. Water is necessary for maintaining metabolism.

- Organisms need oxygen to release the energy contained in their food. Plants, algae, and some bacteria also need carbon dioxide.

- Organisms must have a place to live where they can obtain the things they need.

SECTION 3

Vocabulary

protein *(p. 10)*

carbohydrate *(p. 11)*

lipid *(p. 12)*

phospholipid *(p. 12)*

nucleic acid *(p. 13)*

ATP *(p. 13)*

Section Notes

- Proteins, carbohydrates, lipids, nucleic acids, and ATP are important to life.

- Cells use carbohydrates for energy storage. Carbohydrates are made of sugars.

- Fats and oils store energy. Phospholipids make cell membranes.

- Proteins are made up of amino acids and have many important functions. Enzymes are proteins that help chemical reactions occur quickly.

- Nucleic acids are made up of nucleotides. DNA is a nucleic acid that contains the information for making proteins.

- Cells use molecules of ATP to fuel their activities.

Labs

The Best-Bread Bakery Dilemma *(p. 134)*

Chapter Review

USING VOCABULARY

To complete the following sentences, choose the correct term from each pair of terms listed below:

1. The process of maintaining a stable internal environment is known as ___?___. (*metabolism* or *homeostasis*)

2. The resemblance of offspring to their parents is a result of ___?___. (*heredity* or *stimuli*)

3. A ___?___ obtains food by eating other organisms. (*producer* or *consumer*)

4. Starch is a ___?___ and is made up of ___?___. (*carbohydrate/sugars* or *nucleic acid/nucleotides*)

5. Fats and oils are ___?___ that store energy for an organism. (*proteins* or *lipids*)

UNDERSTANDING CONCEPTS

Multiple Choice

6. Cells are
   a. the structures that contain all of the materials necessary for life.
   b. found in all organisms.
   c. sometimes specialized for particular functions.
   d. All of the above

7. Which of the following is a true statement about all living things?
   a. They cannot sense changes in their external environment.
   b. They have one or more cells.
   c. They do not need to use energy.
   d. They reproduce asexually.

8. Organisms must have food because
   a. food is a source of energy.
   b. food supplies cells with oxygen.
   c. organisms never make their own food.
   d. All of the above

9. A change in an organism's environment that affects the organism's activities is a
   a. response.   c. metabolism.
   b. stimulus.   d. producer.

10. Organisms store energy in
    a. nucleic acids.   c. lipids.
    b. phospholipids.   d. water.

11. The molecule that contains the information on how to make proteins is
    a. ATP.
    b. a carbohydrate.
    c. DNA.
    d. a phospholipid.

12. The subunits of nucleic acids are
    a. nucleotides.   c. sugars.
    b. oils.   d. amino acids.

Short Answer

13. What is the difference between asexual reproduction and sexual reproduction?

14. In one or two sentences, explain why living things must have air.

15. What is ATP, and why is it important to a cell?

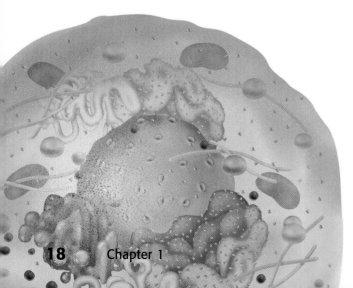

Concept Mapping

16. Use the following terms to create a concept map: cell, carbohydrates, protein, enzymes, DNA, sugars, lipids, nucleotides, amino acids, nucleic acid.

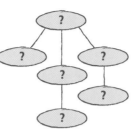

Write one or two sentences to answer the following questions:

17. A flame can move, grow larger, and give off heat. Is a flame alive? Explain.

18. Based on what you know about carbohydrates, lipids, and proteins, why is it important for you to eat a balanced diet?

19. Your friend tells you that the stimulus of music makes his goldfish swim faster. How would you design a controlled experiment to test your friend's claim?

MATH IN SCIENCE

20. An elephant has a mass of 3,900 kg. If 70 percent of the elephant's mass comes from water, how many kilograms of water does the elephant contain?

INTERPRETING GRAPHICS

Take a look at the pictures below, which show the same plant over a time span of 3 days.

Day 1

Day 2

Day 3

21. What is the plant doing?

22. What characteristic(s) of living things is the plant exhibiting?

Reading Check-up

Take a minute to review your answers to the Pre-Reading Questions found at the bottom of page 2. Have your answers changed? If necessary, revise your answers based on what you have learned since you began this chapter.

Life on Mars?

In late 1996 the headlines read, "Evidence of Life on Mars." What kind of life? Aliens similar to those that we see in sci-fi movies? Some creature completely unlike any we've seen before? Not quite, but the story behind the headlines is no less fascinating!

An Unusual Spaceship

In 1996, a group of researchers led by NASA scientists studied a 3.8-billion-year-old meteorite named ALH84001. These scientists agree that ALH84001 is a potato-sized piece of the planet Mars. They also agree that it fell to Earth about 13,000 years ago. It was discovered in Antarctica in 1984. And according to the NASA team, ALH84001 brought with it evidence that life once existed on Mars.

Life-Form Leftovers

On the surface of ALH84001, scientists found certain kinds of *organic molecules* (molecules containing carbon). These molecules are similar to those left behind when living things break down substances for food. And when these scientists examined the interior of the meteorite, they found the same organic

▲ *This scanning electron micrograph image of a tube-like structure found within meteorite ALH84001 is thought to be evidence of life on Mars.*

molecules throughout. Because these molecules were spread throughout the meteorite, scientists concluded the molecules were not contamination from Earth. The NASA team believes these organic leftovers are strong evidence that tiny organisms similar to bacteria lived, ate, and died on Mars millions of years ago.

Dirty Water or Star Dust

Many scientists disagree that ALH84001 contains evidence of Martian life. Some of them argue that the organic compounds are contaminants from Antarctic meltwater that seeped into the meteorite.

Others argue that the molecules were created by processes involving very high temperatures. These scientists think the compounds were formed during star formation and ended up on Mars when it became a planet. Other supporters of this theory believe that the compounds were created during the formation of rocks on Mars. In either case, they argue that no life-forms could exist at such high temperatures and that these compounds could not be the result of living things.

The Debate Continues

Scientists continue to debate the evidence of ALH84001. They are looking for evidence specific to biological life, such as proteins, nucleic acids, and cellular walls. Other scientists are looking to Mars itself for more evidence. Some hope to find underground water that might have supported life. Others hope to gather soil and rock samples that might hold evidence that Mars was once a living planet. Until scientists have more evidence, the debate will continue.

Think About It

▶ If you went to Mars, what kinds of evidence would you look for to prove that life once existed there? How could the discovery of nucleic or amino acids prove life existed on Mars?

Science Fiction

"They're Made Out of Meat"

by Terry Bisson

Two space travelers millions of light-years from home are visiting an uncharted sector of the universe to find signs of life. Their mission is to contact, welcome, and log any and all beings in this quadrant of the universe. Once they discover a living being, they must find a way to communicate with it.

During their mission they encounter a life-form quite unlike anything they have ever seen before. These unusual beings can think and communicate. They have even built a few simple machines, so they aren't exactly pond scum.

Nevertheless, the explorers have very strong doubts about adding this new species to the list of known life-forms in the universe. The creatures are just too strange and, well, disgusting. They just don't fit on the list. Besides, with their limited abilities, it is unlikely they will make contact with any of the other life-forms that dwell elsewhere in the universe.

Perhaps it might be better if the explorers agreed to pretend that they never encountered these beings at all. But the travelers' official duty is to contact and welcome all life-forms, no matter how ugly they are or what they are made of. Can they bring themselves to perform their official duty? Will anyone believe their story if they do?

You'll find out by reading Terry Bisson's short story "They're Made Out of Meat." This story is in the *Holt Anthology of Science Fiction.*

Bacteria and Viruses

Sections

1. Bacteria 24
   MathBreak 24
   QuickLab 26
   Internet Connect 28

2. Bacteria's Role in
   the World 29
   Apply 31

3. Viruses 33
   MathBreak 33
   Chemistry Connection . 34
   Internet Connect 35

Chapter Lab 36
Chapter Review 40
Feature Articles 42, 43
LabBook 136

Pre-Reading Questions

1. How many cells make up a bacterium?

2. What do cheese and yogurt have to do with bacteria?

3. Do you think a virus is alive? Explain your answer.

BACTERIA: FRIEND AND FOE!!

Bacteria are everywhere. Some provide us with medicines and some make foods we eat. Others, like the one pictured here, can cause illnesses. This bacterium is a kind of *Salmonella*, and it can cause food poisoning. *Salmonella* can live inside chickens and other birds. Cooking eggs and chicken properly helps make sure that you don't get sick from *Salmonella*. In this chapter, you will learn more about bacteria and viruses.

OUR CONSTANT COMPANIONS

Bacteria are everywhere. They are in the soil, in the air, and even inside you. When grown in a laboratory, microscopic bacteria form colonies that you can see. In this activity, you will see some of the bacteria that share your world.

Procedure

1. Get **three plastic Petri dishes** containing **nutrient agar** from your teacher. Label one dish "Hand," another "Breath," and another "Soil." Wipe your finger across the inside of the first dish. Breathe into the second dish. Place a small amount of **soil** into the third dish.

2. Secure the Petri dish lids with **transparent tape.** Wash your hands. Place the dishes in a warm, dark place for about 1 week. **Caution:** Do not open the Petri dishes after they are sealed.

3. Observe the Petri dishes each day. What do you see? Record your observations in your ScienceLog.

Analysis

4. How does the appearance of the agar in each dish differ?

5. Which source had the most bacterial growth—your hand, your breath, or the soil? Why do you think this might be?

What You'll Do

◆ Describe the characteristics of a prokaryotic cell.

◆ Explain how bacteria reproduce.

◆ Compare and contrast eubacteria and archaebacteria.

Bacteria

Bacteria are the smallest and simplest organisms on the planet. They are also the most abundant. A single gram of soil (which is about equal to the mass of your pencil eraser) can contain over 2.5 billion bacteria!

Not all bacteria are that small. The largest known bacteria are a thousand times larger than the *average* bacterium. Can you imagine an animal a thousand times larger than you? The first giant bacteria ever identified were found in the intestines of a surgeonfish like the one in **Figure 1.**

Figure 1 *The giant bacteria inside this fish are 0.6 mm long. That's big enough to be seen with the naked eye.*

MATH BREAK

Airborne Organisms

Air typically has around 4,000 bacteria per cubic meter. Cindy's bedroom is 3 m long and 4 m wide. Her ceiling is 2.5 m high. That means there are 30 m³ in her bedroom (3 m × 4 m × 2.5 m). About how many bacteria are in her bedroom's air? About how many bacteria are in the air of your classroom?

Classifying Bacteria

All organisms fit into one of the six kingdoms: Protista, Plantae, Fungi, Animalia, Eubacteria, and Archaebacteria. Bacteria make up the kingdoms Eubacteria (YOO bak TIR ee uh) and Archaebacteria (AHR kee bak TIR ee uh). These two kingdoms contain the oldest forms of life on Earth. In fact, for over 2 billion years, they were the *only* forms of life on Earth.

Look, Mom! No Nucleus! Bacteria are single-celled organisms that do not have nuclei. A cell with no nucleus is called a *prokaryote*. A prokaryote is able to use cellular respiration, move around, and reproduce. Because a prokaryote has these abilities, it can function as an independent organism.

Bacterial Reproduction

Most bacteria reproduce by a type of simple cell division known as **binary fission**, illustrated in **Figures 2** and **3**. In binary fission, a prokaryote's DNA is replicated before cell division. The DNA and its copy attach to the inside of the cell membrane. As the cell grows and the membrane grows longer, the loops of DNA become separated. When the cell is about double in size, the membrane pinches inward. A new cell wall forms, separating the two new cells and their DNA.

Figure 2 Binary Fission

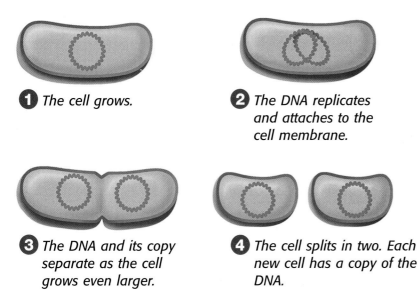

❶ *The cell grows.*

❷ *The DNA replicates and attaches to the cell membrane.*

❸ *The DNA and its copy separate as the cell grows even larger.*

❹ *The cell splits in two. Each new cell has a copy of the DNA.*

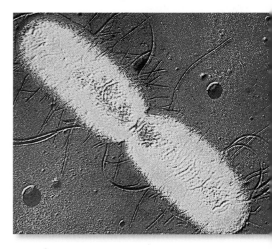

Figure 3 *This bacterium is about to complete binary fission.*

Endospores Each species of bacteria reproduces best at a certain temperature and with a certain amount of moisture. Most species thrive in warm, moist environments. If the environment is unfavorable, some species will be unable to survive. Others will survive by growing a thick protective membrane. These bacteria are then called **endospores.**

Many endospores can survive boiling, freezing, and extremely dry environments. When conditions become favorable again, the endospores will break open, and the bacteria will become active. Scientists have found endospores in the digestive tract of an insect that had been preserved in amber for 30 million years. A similar piece of amber can be seen in **Figure 4.** When the endospores were moistened in a laboratory, the bacteria began to grow!

Figure 4 *Endospores found in a preserved insect indicate that bacteria can survive for millions of years.*

The Shape of Bacteria

Almost all bacteria have a rigid cell wall that gives the organism its characteristic shape. Bacteria have a great variety of shapes. The three most common shapes are illustrated below. Each shape provides a different advantage. Can you guess what the advantage of each shape might be?

Whipping Something Up Some bacteria have hairlike structures called flagella (singular, *flagellum*) that help them move around. *Flagellum* means "whip" in Latin. A flagellum spins like a corkscrew, propelling a bacterium through liquid.

The Most Common Shapes of Bacteria

◀ *Bacilli* (buh SIL ie) *are rod-shaped bacteria. Rod-shaped bacteria have a large surface area, which helps them absorb nutrients, but they can also dry out easily.*

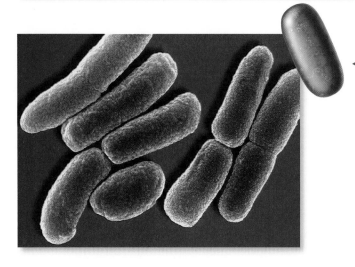

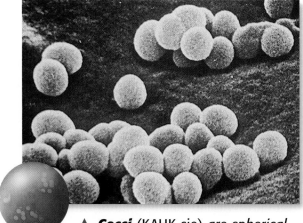

▲ *Cocci* (KAHK sie) *are spherical bacteria. They are more resistant to drying out than rod-shaped bacteria.*

▲ *Spirilla* (spie RI luh) *are long, spiral-shaped bacteria. This is the least common shape for a bacterium. Spirilla move easily in a corkscrew motion, using flagella at both ends.*

Kingdom Eubacteria

Most bacteria are eubacteria. The kingdom Eubacteria has more individual organisms than any of the other five kingdoms. Eubacteria have existed for over 3.5 billion years.

Eu Are What Eu Eat Eubacteria are classified by the way they get food. *Consumers* obtain nutrients from other organisms. Most eubacteria, like those helping to decay the leaf in **Figure 5,** are consumers. Many consumers are *decomposers,* which feed on dead organic matter. Other consumers are *parasitic,* which means they invade the body of another organism to obtain food.

Eubacteria that make their own food are *producers.* Some producers are photosynthetic. Like green plants, they convert the energy of the sun into food. These bacteria contain the green pigment *chlorophyll* that is needed for photosynthesis.

Plant Predecessor? Some bacterial producers are *cyanobacteria* (SIE uh noh bak TIR ee uh). Cyanobacteria live in many different types of water environments, such as the one shown in **Figure 6.** It may be that billions of years ago photosynthetic bacteria similar to these began to live inside certain cells with nuclei. The photosynthetic bacteria made food, and the host provided a protected environment for the bacteria. This might be how the first plants came to be.

Figure 5 *Decomposers, like the ones helping to decay this leaf, return nutrients to the ecosystem.*

✓ Self-Check

Cyanobacteria were once classified as plants. Can you explain why? *(See page 168 to check your answer.)*

Figure 6 *Cyanobacteria in this hot spring excrete chemicals that help form the chalky terraces.*

Kingdom Archaebacteria

Archaebacteria thrive in places where no other living things are found. Scientists have found archaebacteria in the hot springs at Yellowstone National Park and beneath 430 m of ice in Antarctica. They have even been found living 8 km below the Earth's surface!

Archaebacteria are genetically different from eubacteria. Not all archaebacteria have cell walls. The cell walls of archaebacteria—when they do have them—are chemically different from those of all other organisms.

Pass the Salt There are three main types of archaebacteria: methane makers, heat lovers, and salt lovers. Methane makers excrete methane gas. They are found in many places including swamps. Heat lovers live in places like ocean rift vents where temperatures are over 360°C. Salt lovers live in places where the concentration of salt is very high, such as the Dead Sea, shown in **Figure 7.**

Figure 7 *The Dead Sea is so salty that only archaebacteria can survive in it. Fish carried into the Dead Sea by the Jordan River die instantly.*

internetconnect

SC/LINKS
NSTA

TOPIC: Bacteria, Archaebacteria
GO TO: www.scilinks.org
sci*LINKS NUMBER: HSTL230, HSTL235

SECTION REVIEW

1. Draw and label the three main shapes of bacteria.

2. Describe the four steps of binary fission.

3. How do eubacteria and archaebacteria differ?

4. **Analyzing Concepts** Many bacteria cannot reproduce in cooler temperatures and are destroyed at high temperatures. How do humans take advantage of this when preparing and storing food?

Terms to Learn

bioremediation
antibiotic
pathogenic bacteria

What You'll Do

◆ Explain why life on Earth depends on bacteria.
◆ List five ways bacteria are useful to people.
◆ Describe why some bacteria are harmful to people.

Bacteria's Role in the World

Bacteria may be invisible to us, but their effects on the planet are not. Because many types of bacteria cause disease, bacteria have gotten a bad reputation. However, they also do many things that are important to humans.

Good for the Environment

Life as we know it could not exist without bacteria. They are vital to our environment, and we benefit from them in several ways.

Nitrogen-Fixing Nitrogen is an essential chemical for all organisms because it is a component of proteins and DNA. Plants must have nitrogen in order to grow properly. You might think getting nitrogen would be easy because nitrogen gas makes up more than 75 percent of the air. But most plants cannot use nitrogen from the air. They need to take in a different form of nitrogen. *Nitrogen-fixing bacteria* consume nitrogen in the air and change it into a form that plants can use. This process is described in **Figure 8.**

Figure 8 Bacteria's Role in the Nitrogen Cycle.

Recycling Have you ever seen dead leaves and twigs on a forest floor? The leaves and twigs will be recycled over time with the help of bacteria. By breaking down dead organic matter, decomposing bacteria make nutrients available again to living things.

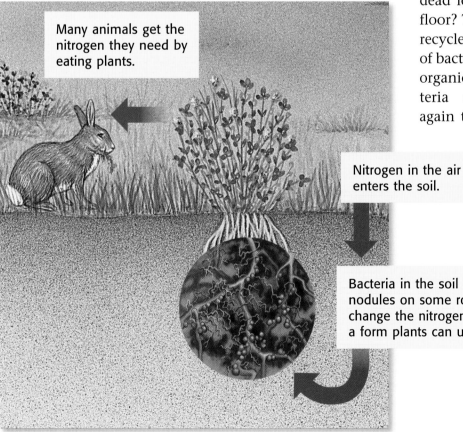

Many animals get the nitrogen they need by eating plants.

Nitrogen in the air enters the soil.

Bacteria in the soil and in nodules on some roots change the nitrogen into a form plants can use.

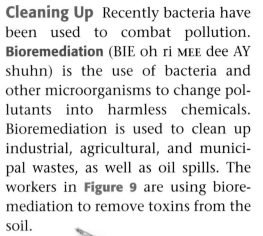

Cleaning Up Recently bacteria have been used to combat pollution. **Bioremediation** (BIE oh ri MEE dee AY shuhn) is the use of bacteria and other microorganisms to change pollutants into harmless chemicals. Bioremediation is used to clean up industrial, agricultural, and municipal wastes, as well as oil spills. The workers in **Figure 9** are using bioremediation to remove toxins from the soil.

Figure 9 *Bioremediating bacteria are added to soil to consume pollutants and excrete them as harmless chemicals.*

Figure 10 *Genes from the Xenopus frog were used to produce the first genetically engineered bacteria.*

Good for People

Scientists are constantly searching for new ways to use bacteria to better the lives of humans. People have been able to genetically engineer bacteria since 1973. It was then that researchers inserted genes from a frog like the one in **Figure 10** into the bacterium *Escherichia coli* (ES uhr RI shee uh COHL ie). The bacterium started reproducing the frog genes. Never before had such a genetically altered organism existed.

Now scientists can genetically engineer bacteria for many purposes, including the production of medicines, insecticides, cleansers, adhesives, foods, and many other products.

Fighting Bacteria with Bacteria Although some bacteria cause diseases, others make chemicals that treat diseases. **Antibiotics** are medicines used to kill bacteria and other microorganisms. Many bacteria have been genetically engineered to make antibiotics in large quantities.

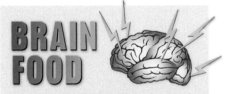

BRAIN FOOD

Alexander Fleming, the Scottish scientist who discovered antibiotics, created a microbial growth shaped like the British flag in honor of the queen's visit to his lab. She was *not* amused.

Ingenious Engineering!

Ralph specializes in genetically engineering bacteria. He has engineered many different types of bacteria to help solve medical and environmental problems, but today he is completely out of ideas. He needs you to help him think of a design for a new bacterium that will either treat a disease or help the environment. What would you want this new bacterium to do? What kinds of traits would you give it?

Insulin Scientists have created genetically engineered bacteria that can produce other medicines, such as insulin. Insulin is a substance needed by the body to properly use sugars and other carbohydrates. People who have *diabetes* cannot produce the insulin they need. They must take insulin daily. In the late 1970s, scientists put genes carrying the genetic code for human insulin into *E. coli* bacteria. The bacteria produced human insulin, which can be separated from the bacteria and given to diabetics.

Feeding Time! Believe it or not, people breed bacteria for food! Every time you eat cheese, yogurt, buttermilk, or sour cream, you also eat a lot of lactic-acid bacteria. *Lactic-acid bacteria* digest the milk sugar lactose and convert it into lactic acid. The lactic acid acts as a preservative and adds flavor to the food. The foods in **Figure 11** could not be made without bacteria.

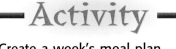

Create a week's meal plan without any foods made with bacteria. What would your diet be like without prokaryotes?

TRY at HOME

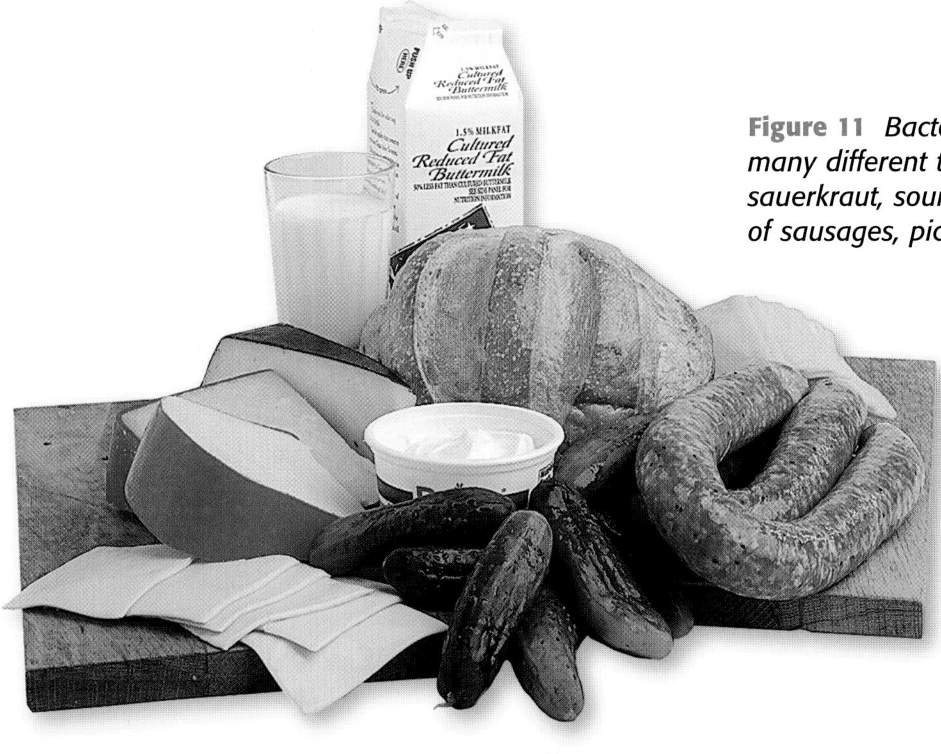

Figure 11 *Bacteria are used to make many different types of food, including sauerkraut, sourdough bread, some kinds of sausages, pickles, and dairy products.*

Harmful Bacteria

We couldn't survive without bacteria, but they are also capable of doing incredible damage. Scientists realized in the mid-1800s that some bacteria are pathogenic. **Pathogenic bacteria** cause diseases, such as the one illustrated in **Figure 12.** These bacteria invade a host organism and obtain nutrients from the host's cells. In the process, they cause damage to the host. Today, almost all bacterial diseases can be treated with antibiotics. Many can also be prevented with vaccines. Some diseases caused by bacteria are shown in the table below.

Figure 12 *Between the years 1346 and 1350, the bubonic plague killed 25 million people. That was one-third of Europe's population at the time.*

Bacterial Diseases

- Dental cavities
- Ulcers
- Strep throat
- Food poisoning
- Bacterial pneumonia
- Lyme disease
- Tuberculosis
- Leprosy
- Typhoid fever
- Bubonic plague

Enough Diseases to Go Around Bacteria cause diseases in other organisms as well as in people. Have you ever seen a plant with discolored spots or soft rot? If so, you've seen bacterial damage to another organism.

Pathogenic bacteria attack plants, animals, protists, fungi, and even other bacteria. They can cause considerable damage to grain, fruit, and vegetable crops. The branch of a pear tree in **Figure 13** shows the effects of pathogenic bacteria.

Figure 13 *This branch of a pear tree has fire blight, a bacterial disease.*

SECTION REVIEW

1. List three different products bacteria are used to make.

2. What are two ways that bacteria affect plants?

3. How can bacteria both cause and cure diseases?

4. **Analyzing Relationships** Describe some of the problems humans would face if there were no bacteria.

What You'll Do

◆ Explain how viruses are similar to and different from living things.

◆ List the four major virus shapes.

◆ Describe the two kinds of viral reproduction.

MATH BREAK

Sizing Up a Virus

If you enlarged an average virus 600,000 times, it would be about the size of a small pea. How tall would you be if you were enlarged 600,000 times?

Viruses

Viruses have been called the greatest threat to the survival of humanity. But what are they? A **virus** is a microscopic particle that invades a cell and often destroys it. They are everywhere, and for humans they are mostly one big headache. That's because many diseases are caused by viruses, including the common cold, flu, and acquired immune deficiency syndrome (AIDS). AIDS is caused by the human immunodeficiency virus (HIV).

It's a Small World

Viruses are incredibly tiny. They are even smaller than the smallest bacteria. About 5 billion of them can fit into a single drop of blood. Because of viruses' small size and ever-changing nature, scientists don't know how many types of viruses exist. The number may be in the billions or higher!

Are They Living?

Like living things, viruses contain protein and nucleic acids. But viruses, such as the ones shown in **Figure 14,** don't eat, grow, breathe, or perform other biological functions. A virus cannot "live" on its own, although it can reproduce inside a living organism that serves as its host. A **host** is an organism that supports a parasite. Using a host's cell as a miniature factory, viruses instruct the cell to produce viruses rather than healthy new cells.

Figure 14 *Viruses are not cells. They do not have cytoplasm or organelles.*

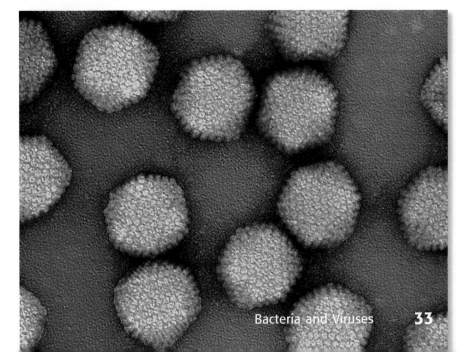

Chemistry

C O N N E C T I O N

Many viruses can form crystalline structures. This is a property of chemicals, not cellular organisms.

Classifying Viruses

Viruses can be grouped by the type of disease they cause, their life cycle, or the type of genetic material they contain. Viruses can also be classified by their basic shape, as illustrated below. No matter what its structure is, every virus is basically some form of genetic material enclosed in a protein coat.

The Basic Shapes of Viruses

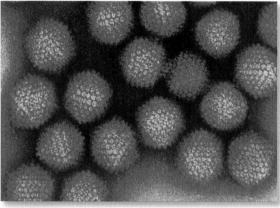

 ▲ **Crystals** The polio virus is shaped like the crystals shown here.

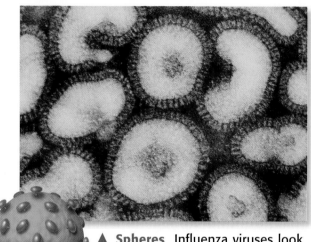 ▲ **Spheres** Influenza viruses look like spheres. HIV is another virus with this structure.

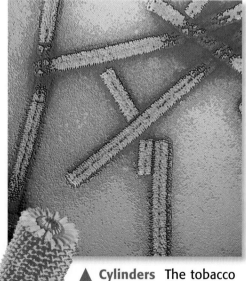 ▲ **Cylinders** The tobacco mosaic virus is cylinder-shaped and attacks tobacco plants.

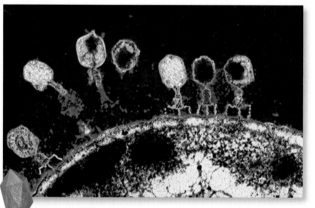 ▲ **Spacecraft** One group of viruses attacks only bacteria. Many of these look almost like spacecraft.

A Destructive House Guest

The one function that viruses share with living things is that they reproduce. They do this by infecting living cells and turning them into virus factories. This is called the *lytic cycle,* as shown in **Figure 15.**

Figure 15 The Lytic Cycle

 1 The virus finds a host cell.

2 The virus enters the cell, or in some cases, the virus's genes are injected into the cell.

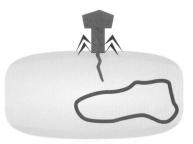

3 Once the virus's genes are inside, they take over the direction of the host cell, turning it into a virus factory.

4 The new viruses break out of the host cell ready to find a new host and repeat the cycle.

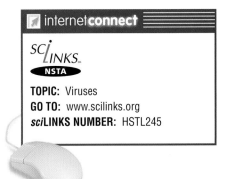

A Ticking Time Bomb Some viruses don't go straight into the lytic cycle. These viruses insert their genes into the host cell, but no new viruses are made immediately. When the host cell divides, each new cell has a copy of the virus's genes. This is called the *lysogenic cycle.* The viral genes can remain inactive for long periods of time until a change in the environment or stress to the organism causes the genes to launch into the lytic cycle.

SECTION REVIEW

1. What would happen if one generation of measles viruses never found a host?

2. Describe the four steps in the lytic cycle.

3. **Analyzing Relationships** Do you think modern transportation has had an effect on the way viruses are spread? Explain your answer.

internetconnect

SCiLINKS

NSTA

TOPIC: Viruses
GO TO: www.scilinks.org
*sci***LINKS NUMBER:** HSTL245

Making Models Lab

Viral Decorations

It's true that viruses are made of only protein and genetic material. But their structures have many different shapes. The shapes help the viruses attach to and get inside of living cells. One viral shape can be made from the template on page 37. In this activity, you will make and modify a model of a virus.

MATERIALS

- virus model template
- construction paper
- colored markers
- scissors
- glue or tape
- pipe cleaners, twist ties, buttons, string, plastic wrap, and recycled or other reusable materials for making variations of the virus

Procedure

1. Carefully copy the virus model template on the next page onto a piece of construction paper. You may make the virus model as large as your teacher allows.

2. Do some research on viruses that have a shape similar to those on this page. Decide how you will change your model. For example, you might want to add the tail and tail fibers of a spacecraft-shaped virus. Or you might wrap the model in plastic to represent the envelope that surrounds the protein coat in HIV.

3. Color your virus model. Cut out your model along the solid black lines. Then fold the virus model along the dotted lines.

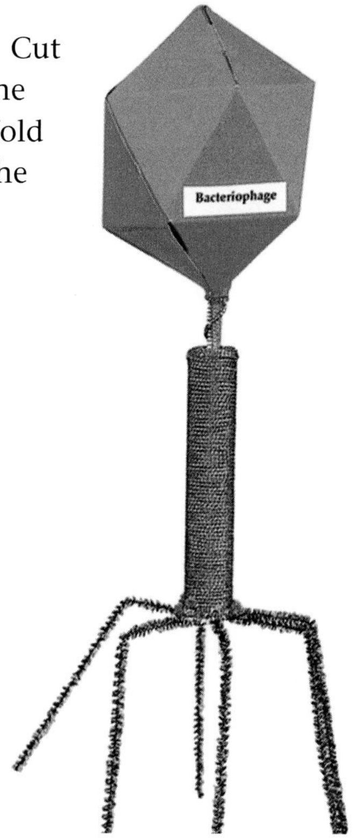

Bacteriophage

Human Immunodeficiency Virus (HIV)

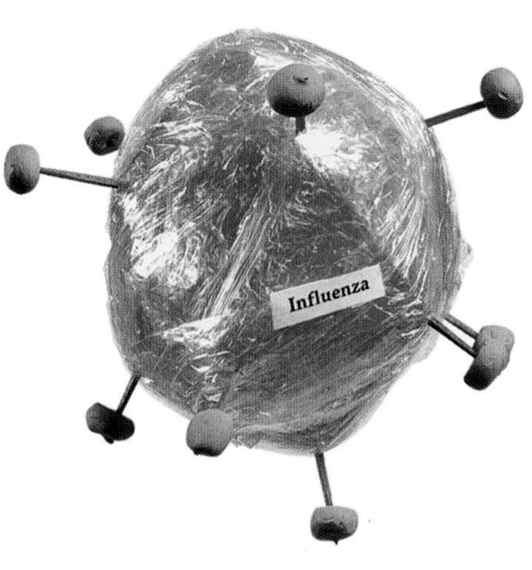

Influenza

4 Glue or tape each lettered tab under the corresponding lettered triangle. For example, glue or tape the large Z tab under the Z-shaded triangle. When you are done, you should have a closed box with 20 sides.

5 Make the changes that you planned in step 2. Write the name of your virus on the model. Decorate your classroom with your virus and those of your classmates.

Analysis

6 Describe the changes you made to your virus model. How do you think the virus might use them?

7 Does your virus cause disease? If so, explain what disease it causes, how it reproduces, and how the virus is spread.

Going Further
Research in the library or on the Internet an unusual virus that causes an illness, such as the influenza virus, HIV, or Ebola virus. Explain what is unusual about the virus, what illness it causes, and how it might be avoided.

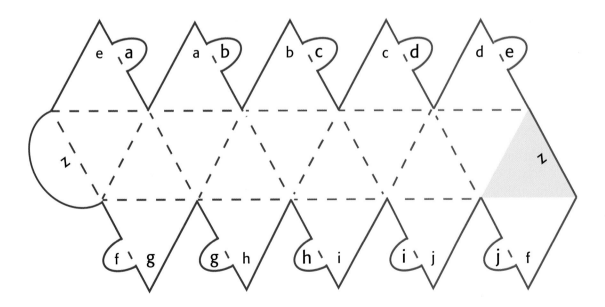

Chapter Highlights

Vocabulary

binary fission *(p. 25)*

endospore *(p. 25)*

Section Notes

- Bacteria are classified as eubacteria or archaebacteria. Both are prokaryotes.

- Most bacteria have one of three shapes. Bacilli are rod-shaped. Cocci are spherical, and spirilla are long, spiral rods.

- Most bacteria reproduce by binary fission. Some produce endospores that can survive for thousands of years.

- Many eubacteria are decomposers. They obtain their energy from dead organic matter. Others are parasites.

- Many bacterial producers, including cyanobacteria, contain chlorophyll.

- Archaebacteria live in places where no other organisms can survive. Many are grouped as salt lovers, methane makers, and heat lovers.

☑ Skills Check

Math Concepts

MULTIPLYING MICROORGANISMS Some bacteria can divide every 20 minutes in an ideal growing environment. That means that if you start out with just one bacterium, in an hour there will be eight bacteria. There will be 512 bacteria in 3 hours, 32,768 in 5 hours, and 1,073,741,824 bacteria in 10 hours!

Visual Understanding

BACTERIA VERSUS VIRUSES The diagrams on pp. 25 and 35 illustrate the way some bacteria and viruses reproduce. Make sure you under-

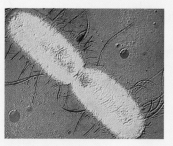

stand how each process works. Viruses use their hosts' cells to reproduce. Think about how this is different from the way pathogenic bacteria use a host's cell.

SECTION 2

Vocabulary

bioremediation *(p. 30)*

antibiotic *(p. 30)*

pathogenic bacteria *(p. 32)*

Section Notes

- Bacteria are important to the planet. Some act as decomposers. Others convert nitrogen gas to a form that plants can use.

- Bacteria are used in making a variety of foods, medicines, and pesticides. They are also used to clean up pollution.

- Pathogenic bacteria cause diseases in humans as well as other organisms.

Labs

Aunt Flossie and the Intruder *(p. 136)*

SECTION 3

Vocabulary

virus *(p. 33)*

host *(p. 33)*

Section Notes

- Viruses have characteristics of both living and nonliving things. They can reproduce only inside a living cell.

- Viruses may be classified by their structure, the kind of disease they cause, or their life cycle.

- In order for a virus to reproduce, it must enter a cell, reproduce itself, and then break open the cell. This is called the lytic cycle.

- The genes of a virus are incorporated into the genes of the host cell in the lysogenic cycle. The virus's genes may remain inactive for years.

Chapter Review

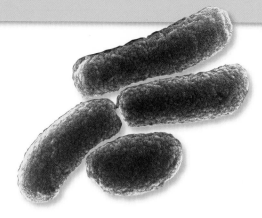

USING VOCABULARY

To complete the following sentences, choose the correct term from each pair of terms listed below:

1. Rod-shaped bacteria are called ___?___. (*bacilli* or *cocci*)

2. Most bacteria reproduce by ___?___. (*endospores* or *binary fission*)

3. Bacterial infections can be treated with ___?___. (*antibiotics* or *bioremediation*)

4. A virus needs a ___?___ to reproduce. (*crystal* or *host*)

5. Without ___?___ bacteria, life on Earth could not exist. (*pathogenic* or *nitrogen-fixing*)

6. ___?___ make their own food. (*Consumers* or *Producers*)

UNDERSTANDING CONCEPTS

Multiple Choice

7. Bacteria are used for all of the following except
   a. making certain foods.
   b. making antibiotics.
   c. cleaning up oil spills.
   d. preserving fruit.

8. In the lytic cycle
   a. the host cell is destroyed.
   b. the host cell destroys the virus.
   c. the host cell becomes a virus.
   d. the host cell undergoes cell division.

9. A bacterial cell
   a. is an endospore.
   b. has a loop of DNA.
   c. has a distinct nucleus.
   d. is a eukaryote.

10. Eubacteria
    a. include methane makers.
    b. include decomposers.
    c. all have chlorophyll.
    d. are all rod-shaped.

11. Cyanobacteria
    a. are consumers.
    b. are parasites.
    c. contain chlorophyll.
    d. are decomposers.

12. Archaebacteria
    a. are a special type of eubacteria.
    b. live only in places without oxygen.
    c. are primarily lactic-acid bacteria.
    d. can live in hostile environments.

13. Viruses
    a. are about the same size as bacteria.
    b. have nuclei.
    c. can reproduce only within a host cell.
    d. don't infect plants.

14. Bacteria are important to the planet as
    a. decomposers of dead organic matter.
    b. processors of nitrogen.
    c. makers of medicine.
    d. All of the above

Short Answer

15. How are the functions of nitrogen-fixing bacteria and decomposers similar?

16. What is the difference between the lytic cycle and the lysogenic cycle?

Concept Mapping

17. Use the following terms to create a concept map: eubacteria, bacilli, cocci, spirilla, parasites, consumers, producers, cyanobacteria.

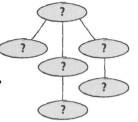

CRITICAL THINKING AND PROBLEM SOLVING

Write one or two sentences to answer the following questions:

18. Describe some of the problems you think bacteria might face if there were no humans.

19. A nuclear power plant explodes and wipes out every living thing within a 30 km radius. What kind of organism do you think might colonize the radioactive area first? Why?

MATH IN SCIENCE

20. An ounce is equal to about 28 g. If 1 g of soil contains 2.5 billion bacteria, how many bacteria are in 1 oz?

21. A bacterial cell infected by a virus divides every 20 minutes. After 10,000 divisions, the virus breaks loose from its host cell. About how many weeks will this take?

INTERPRETING GRAPHICS

The following diagram illustrates the stages of binary fission. Match each statement with the correct stage.

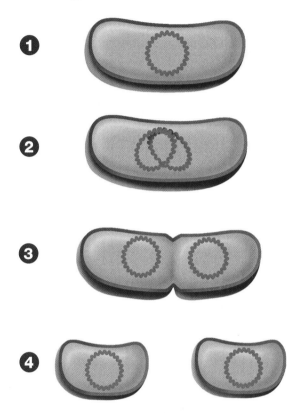

22. The DNA loops separate.

23. The DNA loop replicates.

24. The parent cell starts to expand.

25. The DNA attaches to the cell membrane.

Reading Check-up

Take a minute to review your answers to the Pre-Reading Questions found at the bottom of page 22. Have your answers changed? If necessary, revise your answers based on what you have learned since you began this chapter.

Science, Technology, and Society

Edible Vaccines

No one likes getting a shot, right? Unfortunately, though, shots are a necessary part of life. This is because people in this country are protected from life-threatening diseases by vaccinations. But vaccination shots are expensive, may require refrigeration, and require trained medical professionals to administer them. These facts often keep people in developing countries from getting vaccinated.

▲ *Banana vaccines may soon replace a shot in the arm!*

Pass the Banana, Please

Edible vaccines would have several important advantages over traditional injected vaccines. First of all, they wouldn't require a painful shot! But more important, these vaccines will be cheaper to produce and may not require refrigeration or trained medical professionals. Plants like bananas are easily grown in fields and greenhouses in many Third World countries. One banana could even carry vaccines for several diseases at one time! But just how could a banana do this?

Add Some DNA

Scientists have made DNA that closely resembles the "fingerprints" of specific disease particles. They can insert this DNA into banana genes that code for proteins. Scientists hope they can trick the human immune system into recognizing these proteins as invaders and producing the necessary antibodies to fight diseases. Unlike traditional vaccines, these transgenic bananas (bananas containing foreign DNA) do not carry the risk of infection because they do not contain any viral particles.

Transgenic plants aren't all that new. Agricultural scientists make transgenic plants to improve crops. Scientists have introduced new DNA into fruits and vegetables so that they are more resistant to pests and drought; have larger, sweeter, and more colorful fruit; and ripen more quickly.

Important Questions

Unfortunately, edible vaccines will not be available for several years. Some safety concerns must still be addressed before these vaccines can be given to people. Do edible vaccines have side effects? How long will the resistance last? What happens if someone eats too many bananas? Research labs are testing the vaccines to answer these questions.

Check It Out!

▶ The milk of transgenic animals is also being tested as a potential vaccine carrier. Scientists hope that goat's milk containing malarialike proteins will prevent as many as 3 million deaths each year. Investigate for yourself how the malaria vaccine will work.

Helpful Viruses

Less than 100 years ago, people had no way to treat bacterial infections. If you became ill from contact with pathogenic bacteria, you could only hope that your immune system would be able to defeat the invaders. But in 1928 a Scottish scientist named Alexander Fleming discovered the first antibiotic, or bacteria-killing drug. This first antibiotic was called penicillin.

Using Viruses to Fight Bacteria

Since Fleming's discovery, people have used antibiotics to treat infections and to purify water supplies. But scientists are now realizing that many bacteria are becoming resistant to existing antibiotics. It is quite possible that the overuse of antibiotics will make all current antibiotics ineffective in the near future. So what will people use to fight bacterial infections? Some scientists think viruses might be the answer! You might be thinking that viruses can only cause diseases, not cure them, but there is a particular type of virus, called a bacteriophage, that attacks only bacteria.

How Do They Do This?

Bacteriophages destroy bacteria cells in the same way other viruses can destroy animal or plant cells. Each kind of bacteriophage can only infect a particular species of bacteria. This can make an extremely effective antibiotic. Existing antibiotics kill not only harmful bacteria but also bacteria that people need to stay healthy. This can make people treated with antibiotics very sick, causing a breakdown in their immune system or digestive process. Because bacteriophages would kill only specific harmful bacteria, using bacteriophages could eliminate antibiotics' damaging side effects.

Current Uses

Bacteriophages are not yet used as antibiotics because the immune system destroys the viruses before they can infect the pathogenic bacteria. Scientists are still researching ways to use bacteriophages effectively.

Bacteriophages are currently used to diagnose bacterial infections quickly. Diagnoses can be made by injecting many different types of bacteriophages into a patient. Blood tests then indicate which virus was able to reproduce, in turn determining the type of bacterial infection the patient has. Scientists are also able to use bacteriophages in the same way to detect bacterial contamination of food and water supplies. Perhaps one day in the future, your doctor will give you a helpful virus instead of an antibiotic to fight the harmful bacteria that make you sick!

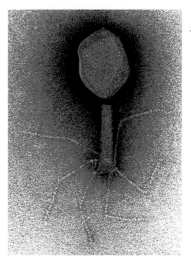

◀ *Some bacteriophages look more like machines than living organisms.*

Going Further

▶ Bacteriophages aren't always so helpful. Sometimes they can do more harm than good. Can you think of ways bacteriophages can cause trouble for humans ?

Protists and Fungi

Sections

1. **Protists** 46
   Chemistry Connection . 50
   Geology Connection . . . 53
   Internet Connect 56

2. **Fungi** 57
   QuickLab 59
   MathBreak 60
   QuickLab 61
   Apply 61
   Internet Connect 63

Chapter Lab 64

Chapter Review 68

Feature Articles 70, 71

Pre-Reading Questions

1. What is seaweed?
2. What is a fungus?
3. Do mushrooms have roots?

HARDWORKING MUSHROOMS!

The kingdoms Protista and Fungi (FUHN JIE) contain many fascinating and beneficial organisms. Protists make most of Earth's oxygen. Many trees and other plants need the help of fungi to get nutrients from the soil. The mushrooms on these pages are fungi that help break down dead plant matter on the forest floor. This process helps recycle the nutrients of the forest. In this chapter, you will learn more about protists and fungi.

Activity

A MICROSCOPIC WORLD

In this activity, you will observe some common protists in pond water or in a solution called a *hay infusion.*

Procedure

1. Using a **plastic eyedropper,** place one drop of **pond water** or **hay infusion** onto a **micro-scope slide.**

2. Add one drop of **ProtoSlo**™ to the drop on the slide.

3. Add a **plastic coverslip** by putting one edge on the slide and then slowly lowering it over the drop to prevent air bubbles.

4. Observe the slide under low power of a **microscope.** Once you've located an organism, try high power for a closer look.

5. In your ScienceLog, sketch the organisms you see under high power.

Analysis

6. How many different organisms do you see?

7. Are the organisms alive? Support your answer with evidence.

8. How many cells does each organism appear to have?

Terms to Learn

protist

funguslike
  protist

parasite

host

algae

phytoplankton

protozoa

What You'll Do

◆ Describe the characteristics of protists.

◆ Name the three groups of protists, and give examples of each.

◆ Explain how protists reproduce.

Protists

Some are so tiny they cannot be seen without a microscope, and others grow many meters long. Some are poisonous, and others provide food. Some are like plants. Some are like animals. And some are nothing like plants or animals. Despite their differences, all of these organisms are related. What are they? They are all members of the kingdom Protista and are called **protists.** Look at **Figure 1** to see some of the variety of protists.

Zooflagellate

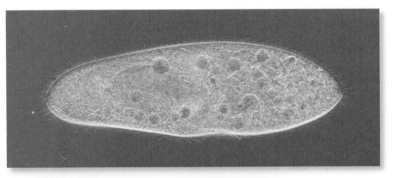

Paramecium

Ulva

Figure 1 *Protists have many different shapes and sizes.*

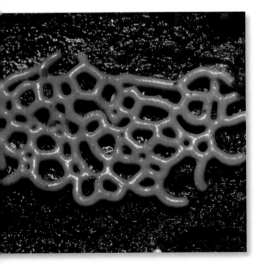

Pretzel slime mold

General Characteristics

All protists are *eukaryotic*. That means their cells have a nucleus. Most protists are single-celled organisms, but some are multicellular. Scientists generally agree that the more complex eukaryotic organisms—plants, animals, and fungi—all originated from primitive protists.

Some protists are *producers*. Like plants, they get their energy from the sun through *photosynthesis*. Others are *consumers*. They cannot obtain energy from sunlight and must get food from their environment. Protists are often classified by the way they obtain energy. This method groups these organisms into funguslike protists, plantlike protists, or animal-like protists.

Funguslike Protists

A fungus is an organism that obtains its food from dead organic matter or from the body of another organism. You will learn more about fungi in the next section. The protists that get food this way are called **funguslike protists.** The funguslike protists are consumers that secrete digestive juices into the food source and then absorb the digested nutrients. These protists also reproduce like fungi. Two types of funguslike protists will be discussed in this chapter—slime molds and water molds.

It's Slime! *Slime molds* are thin masses of living matter. They look like colorful, shapeless globs of slime. Many slime molds live as single-celled organisms. But during times of environmental stress, these single organisms come together to form a group of cells with many nuclei and a single cytoplasm. Slime molds live in cool, shady, moist places in the woods and in fresh water. **Figure 2** shows a slime mold growing over a log.

Slime molds eat bacteria, yeast, and small bits of decaying plant and animal matter. They surround food particles and digest them. As long as food and water are available, a slime mold will continue to grow. It may cover an area more than 1 m across!

When growth conditions are unfavorable, a slime mold develops stalklike structures with rounded knobs at the top. You can see this in **Figure 3.** The knobs contain *spores.* The spores can survive for a long time without water or nutrients. When conditions improve, the spores will develop into new slime molds.

Figure 2 *Slime molds, like this scrambled egg slime mold, are consumers.*

Figure 3 *The spore-containing knobs of a slime mold are called sporangia.*

Moldy Water? Another type of funguslike protist is the *water mold*. Most water molds are small, single-celled organisms. Water molds live in water, moist soil, or other organisms.

Some water molds are *decomposers* and eat dead organic matter. But many water molds are parasites. **Parasites** invade the body of another organism to obtain the nutrients they need. The organism a parasite invades is called a **host**. Hosts can be living plants, animals, algae, or fungi. A parasitic water mold is shown in **Figure 4**.

Some parasitic water molds cause diseases. A water mold causes "late blight" of potatoes, the disease that led to the Great Potato Famine in Ireland from 1845—1852. Another water mold attacks grapes and threatened the French wine industry in the late 1800s. These protists still endanger crops today, but fortunately methods now exist to control them.

Figure 4 *Parasitic water molds attack various organisms, including fish.*

Self-Check

Are all funguslike protists decomposers? Explain. *(See page 168 to check your answers.)*

Plantlike Protists: Algae

A second group of protists are producers. Like plants, they use the sun's energy to make food through photosynthesis. These plantlike protists are also known as **algae** (AL JEE). All algae (singular, *alga*) have the green pigment chlorophyll, which is used for photosynthesis. But most algae also have other pigments that give them a specific color. Almost all algae live in water. You can see some examples of algae in **Figure 5**.

Some algae are multicellular. These algae generally live in shallow water along the shore. You may know these as *seaweed* or *kelp*. Some of these algae can grow to many meters in length.

Figure 5 *Algae range in size from giant seaweeds to single-celled organisms.*

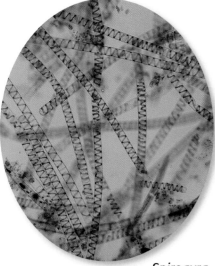

Spirogyra

Kelp

Single-celled algae cannot be seen without a microscope. They usually float near the water's surface. The single-celled algae make up **phytoplankton** (FITE oh PLANK tuhn). Phytoplankton are producers that provide food for most other water-dwelling organisms. They also produce most of the world's oxygen.

The plantlike protists are divided into phyla based on their color and cell structure. We will discuss six of the phyla here: red algae, brown algae, green algae, diatoms, dinoflagellates, and euglenoids.

Red Algae Most of the world's seaweeds are red algae. They contain chlorophyll and a red pigment that gives them their color. These multicellular protists live mainly in tropical marine waters, attached to rocks or other algae. Their red pigment allows them to absorb the light that filters deep into the clear water of the Tropics. Red algae can grow as much as 260 m below the surface of the water but are usually less than 1 m in length.

Brown Algae Most of the seaweeds found in cool climates are brown algae. They attach to rocks or form large floating beds in ocean waters. Brown algae have chlorophyll and a yellow-brown pigment. Many are very large—some grow 60 m in just one growing season! The tops of these gigantic algae are exposed to sunlight. The food made here by photosynthesis is transported to the parts of the algae that are too deep in the water to receive sunlight. An example of a brown alga can be seen in **Figure 6.**

Figure 6 Laminaria *is a brown alga.*

Green Algae The green algae are the most diverse group of plantlike protists. They are green because chlorophyll is the main pigment they contain. Most live in water or moist soil, but others are found in melting snow, on tree trunks, and even inside other organisms.

Many green algae are single-celled, microscopic organisms. Others are multicellular. These species may grow up to 8 m long. Individual cells of some species of green algae live in groups called colonies. **Figure 7** shows colonies of *Volvox.*

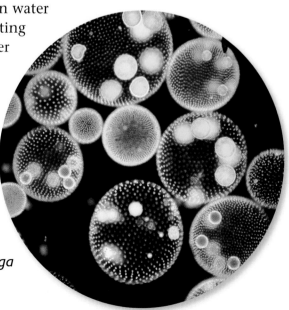

Figure 7 Volvox *is a green alga that grows in round colonies.*

Diatoms Diatoms (DIE e TAHMZ) are single-celled organisms. They are found in both salt water and fresh water. As with all algae, diatoms get their energy from photosynthesis. They make up a large percentage of phytoplankton.

As you can see in **Figure 8,** many diatoms have unusual shapes. Their cell walls contain cellulose and silica, a rigid, glasslike substance. The cells are enclosed in a shell with two parts that fit neatly together. Piles of diatom shells deposited over millions of years form a fine, crumbly substance that is used in silver polish, toothpaste, filters, and insulation.

Figure 8 *Although most diatoms are free floating, many cling to plants, shellfish, sea turtles, and whales.*

Dinoflagellates Most dinoflagellates (DIE noh FLAJ uh lits) are single-celled algae. They live primarily in salt water, although a few species live in fresh water, and some are even found in snow. Dinoflagellates have two whiplike strands called *flagella* (singular, *flagellum*). The beating of these flagella causes the cells to spin through the water. For this reason they are sometimes called spinning flagellates.

Most dinoflagellates get energy from photosynthesis, but a few are consumers, decomposers, or parasites. Some dinoflagellates are red and produce a strong poison. If these algae multiply rapidly, they can turn the water red, causing a dangerous condition known as *red tide*. When shellfish eat these algae, the poison is concentrated in their bodies. The shellfish are then toxic to humans and other vertebrates who eat them. A red tide is shown in **Figure 9.**

Chemistry
C O N N E C T I O N

Some dinoflagellates give off light. A chemical reaction in the cells produces light that is similar to the light produced by fireflies. Water filled with these dinoflagellates glows like a twinkling neon light.

Figure 9 *Red tides occur throughout the world and are common in the Gulf of Mexico.*

Euglenoids Euglenoids (yoo GLEE NOYDZ) are single-celled protists that live primarily in fresh water. Most euglenoids have characteristics of both plants and animals. Like plants, they use photosynthesis. But when light is too low for photosynthesis, they can become consumers, like animals. Euglenoids can also move like animals. Flagella propel the organisms through the water. The structure of a euglenoid is shown in **Figure 10.**

Some euglenoids do not have chloroplasts for photosynthesis. These species either consume other small protists or absorb dissolved nutrients.

Nucleus

Chloroplasts are needed for photosynthesis. These structures contain the green pigment chlorophyll.

Most euglenoids have two **flagella,** one long and one short. The long flagellum is used to move the organism through water.

Euglenoids can't see, but they have **eyespots** that respond to light.

A special structure called a **contractile vacuole** collects excess water and removes it from the cell.

Figure 10 *Euglenoids have both plant and animal characteristics.*

SECTION REVIEW

1. How does a slime mold survive when food and water are limited?

2. Which plantlike protists move? How?

3. Add the following terms to the concept map at right: consumer, water mold, diatom, euglenoid.

4. Look at the picture of a euglenoid on this page. Which cell structures are plantlike? Which are animal-like?

5. **Analyzing Relationships** How do funguslike protists differ from plantlike protists?

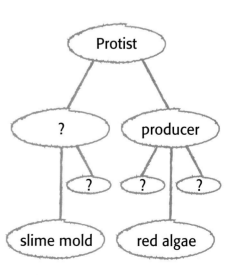

Animal-Like Protists: Protozoa

The animal-like protists are single-celled consumers. These protists are also known as **protozoa.** Some are parasites. Many can move. Scientists do not agree on how to group protozoa, but they are often divided into four phyla: amoebalike protists, flagellates, ciliates, and spore-forming protists.

Amoebalike Protists An amoeba (uh MEE buh) is a soft, jellylike protozoan. Amoebas are found in both fresh and salt water, in soil, or as parasites in animals. Although an amoeba looks shapeless, it is actually a highly structured cell. Like euglenoids, amoebas have contractile vacuoles to get rid of excess water. Amoebas move with *pseudopodia* (soo doh POH dee uh). *Pseudopodia* means "false feet." You can see how an amoeba uses pseudopodia to move in **Figure 11.**

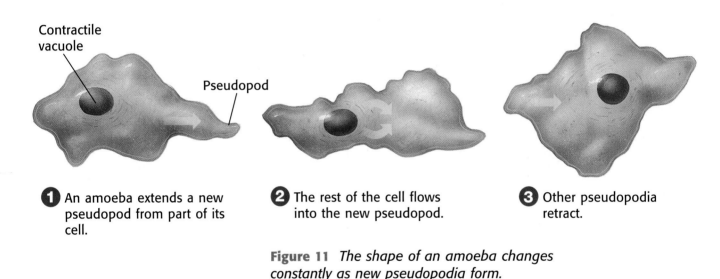

Contractile vacuole

Pseudopod

❶ An amoeba extends a new pseudopod from part of its cell.

❷ The rest of the cell flows into the new pseudopod.

❸ Other pseudopodia retract.

Figure 11 *The shape of an amoeba changes constantly as new pseudopodia form.*

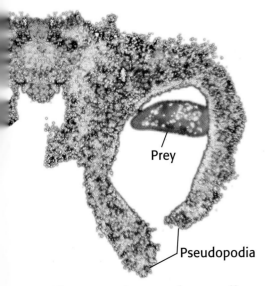

Prey

Pseudopodia

Figure 12 *An amoeba engulfs its prey with its pseudopodia.*

Feeding Amoebas Like slime molds, amoebas feed by engulfing food. An amoeba senses the presence of another single-celled organism and moves toward it. It surrounds a bacterium or small protist with its pseudopodia, forming a *food vacuole.* Enzymes move into the vacuole to digest the food, and the digested food passes out of the vacuole into the cytoplasm of the amoeba. To get rid of wastes, an amoeba reverses the process. A waste-filled vacuole is moved to the edge of the cell and is released. **Figure 12** shows an amoeba feeding.

Some amoebas are parasites. Certain species live in the human intestine and cause amebic dysentery, a painful condition that can involve bleeding ulcers.

Protozoa with Shells Not all amoebalike protozoa look like amoebas. Some have an outer shell. *Radiolarians* (RAY dee oh LER ee uhnz) have shells made of silica that look like glass ornaments. This type of protozoan is shown in **Figure 13**. *Foraminiferans* (fuh RAM uh NIF uhr uhnz) have snail-like shells made of calcium carbonate.

Flagellates Flagellates (FLAJ uh LITS) are protozoa that use flagella to move. The flagella wave back and forth to propel the organism forward. Some flagellates live in water. Others are parasites that can cause disease.

The flagellate parasite, *Giardia lamblia,* lives in the digestive tracts of humans and other vertebrates. This parasite is shown in **Figure 14**. In an inactive form, *Giardia* (JEE ar DEE uh) can survive in water. Hikers or others who drink water infected with *Giardia* can get diarrhea and severe stomach cramps, but the disease is usually not fatal.

Some flagellates live in symbiosis with vertebrates or invertebrates. In *symbiosis,* one organism lives closely with another organism, and each organism helps the other survive. One symbiotic flagellate lives in the guts of termites and digests the cellulose in the wood that the termites eat. Without the protozoa, the termites could not completely digest the cellulose.

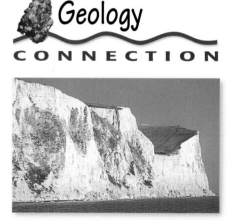

Figure 13 *Radiolarians are amoebalike protozoa with shells.*

Geology
CONNECTION

Foraminiferans have existed for over 600 million years. During this time, the shells of dead foraminiferans have been sinking to the bottom of the ocean. Millions of years ago, foraminiferan shells formed a thick layer of sediment of limestone and chalk deposits. The chalk deposits known as the White Cliffs of Dover in England were formed this way.

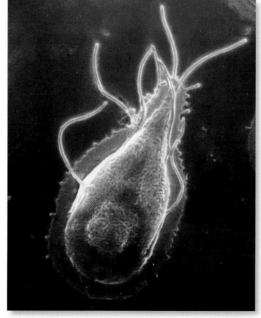

Figure 14 *The parasitic protist,* Giardia lamblia, *is a primitive cell. Can you see why it is a flagellate?*

Ciliates Ciliates (SIL ee its) are the most complex protozoa. Ciliates have hundreds of tiny hairlike structures known as *cilia.* The cilia move a protozoan forward by beating back and forth. Cilia can beat up to 60 times a second! In some species, clumps of cilia form bristlelike structures used for movement. Cilia are also important for feeding. Ciliates use their cilia to sweep food through the water toward them. The best known ciliate is *Paramecium* (PAR uh MEE see uhm), shown in **Figure 15.**

Ciliates have two kinds of nuclei. A large nucleus called a *macronucleus* controls the functions of the cell. A smaller nucleus, the *micronucleus,* passes genetic material to another individual during sexual reproduction.

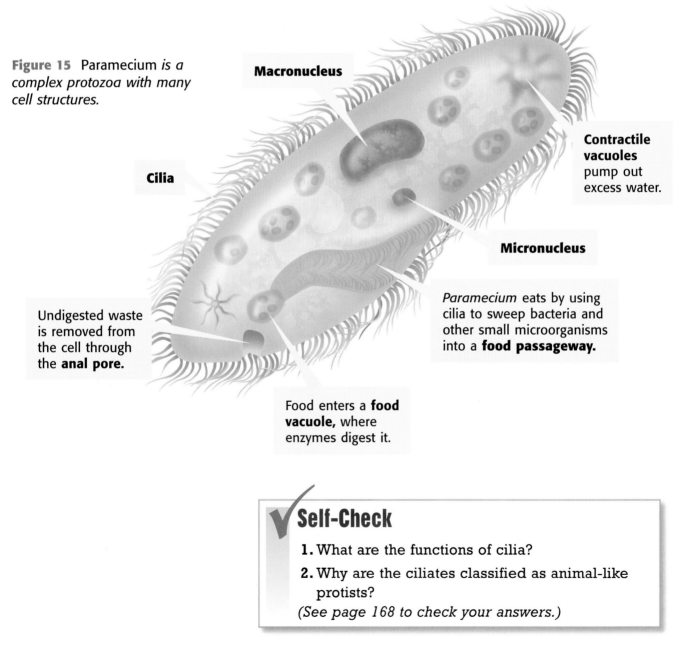

Figure 15 Paramecium *is a complex protozoa with many cell structures.*

Macronucleus

Cilia

Contractile vacuoles pump out excess water.

Micronucleus

Undigested waste is removed from the cell through the **anal pore.**

Paramecium eats by using cilia to sweep bacteria and other small microorganisms into a **food passageway.**

Food enters a **food vacuole,** where enzymes digest it.

✓ Self-Check

1. What are the functions of cilia?
2. Why are the ciliates classified as animal-like protists?

(See page 168 to check your answers.)

Spore-Forming Protists The spore-forming protozoa are all parasites that absorb nutrients from their hosts. They have no cilia or flagella, and they cannot move on their own. Spore-forming protozoa have complicated life cycles that usually involve two or more different hosts.

Plasmodium (plaz MOH dee uhm) *vivax* (VIE VAKS) is the spore-forming protist that causes malaria. Malaria is a serious disease that is carried by mosquitoes in tropical areas. Although malaria can be treated with drugs, more than 2 million people die from malaria each year.

The Life Cycle of *Plasmodium vivax*

Plasmodium vivax is a parasite that has two different hosts, mosquitoes and humans. It needs both hosts to survive. Once a human is bitten by an infected mosquito, *Plasmodium* spores enter the liver. The spores multiply and change form.

They then enter red blood cells and multiply, causing the red blood cells to burst. If the malaria victim is bitten by another mosquito, the disease can then be carried to another human.

1 A mosquito infected with *P. vivax* bites a human, delivering spores.

2 The spores infect human liver cells, reproduce, and enter the bloodstream from the liver.

6 The spores move into the mosquito's mouth.

3 The *P. vivax* invade red blood cells and multiply rapidly. The red blood cells burst.

5 The *P. vivax* grow in the mosquito's gut and release large numbers of spores.

4 A mosquito bites a human and picks up the *P. vivax*.

Reproduction of Protists

Some protists reproduce asexually. In asexual reproduction, the offspring come from just one parent. Both animal-like amoebas and plantlike *Euglena* reproduce asexually by fission, as shown in **Figure 16.**

Some protists can also reproduce sexually. Sexual reproduction requires two parents. Animal-like *Paramecium* sometimes reproduces sexually by a process called conjugation. During conjugation, two *Paramecium* join together and exchange genetic material using their micronuclei. Then they divide to produce four organisms with new combinations of genetic material. Conjugation is shown in **Figure 17.**

Many protists reproduce both asexually and sexually. In some algae, asexual reproduction and sexual reproduction alternate from one generation to the next.

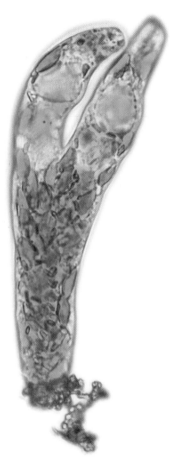

Figure 16 *During fission, Euglena divides lengthwise.*

Figure 17 *Conjugation in* Paramecium *is a type of sexual reproduction.*

SECTION REVIEW

1. Name the three main groups of protists, and give the characteristics of each.

2. What are three ways that flagella and cilia differ?

3. **Making Inferences** Killing mosquitoes is one method of controlling malaria. Using what you know about the organism that causes malaria, explain why this method works.

Terms to Learn

fungus   spore
hyphae   mold
mycelium   lichen

What You'll Do

◆ Describe the characteristics of fungi.
◆ Distinguish between the four main groups of fungi.
◆ Describe how fungi can be helpful or harmful.
◆ Define *lichen*.

Fungi

Have you ever heard someone say, "A fungus is among us"? This statement has more truth in it than you may realize. The mushrooms on pizza are a type of fungus (plural, *fungi*). The yeast used to make bread is a fungus. Fungi are also used to produce cheeses, antibiotics, and soy sauce. And if you've ever had athlete's foot, you can thank a fungus. Fungi are everywhere!

Characteristics of Fungi

Fungi are eukaryotic consumers, but they are so different from other organisms that they are placed in their own kingdom. As you can see in **Figure 18,** fungi come in a variety of shapes, sizes, and colors. But all fungi have similar ways of obtaining food and reproducing.

Figure 18 *Fungi vary in their size and shape.*

Bird's nest fungus

Witch's hat fungus

Ascomycetus

Straight coral fungus

Food for Fungi   Fungi are consumers, but they cannot eat or engulf food. Fungi must live on or near their food supply. Most fungi obtain nutrients by secreting digestive juices onto a food source, then absorbing the dissolved substances. Many fungi are *decomposers*. This means that they feed on dead plant or animal matter. Other fungi are parasites.

Some fungi live in symbiotic relationships with other organisms. For example, many types of fungi grow on the roots of plants. They release an acid that changes minerals in the soil into forms that plants can use. The fungi also protect the plant from some disease-causing organisms.

Self-Check

1. In what ways are fungi and fungus-like protists alike?

2. How are hyphae and mycelia related?

(See page 168 to check your answer.)

Hidden from View All fungi are made of eukaryotic cells, which have nuclei. Some fungi are single-celled, but most fungi are multicellular. Multicellular fungi are made up of chains of cells called **hyphae** (HIE fee). Hyphae are fungal filaments that are similar to plant roots. These filaments are made of cells. But unlike plant root cells, the hyphae cells have openings in their cell walls that allow cytoplasm to move freely between the cells. The hyphae grow together to form a twisted mass called the **mycelium** (mie SEE lee uhm). The mycelium is the major part of the fungus, but it is often hidden from view underneath the ground. **Figure 19** shows the hyphae and mycelium of a fungus.

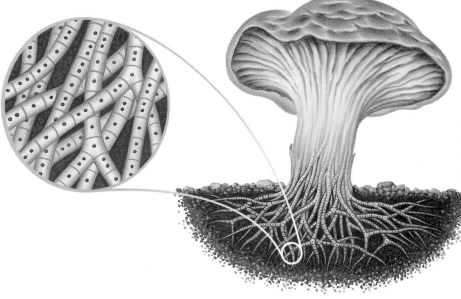

Figure 19 *The mycelium of a fungus is formed by hyphae and is often underground.*

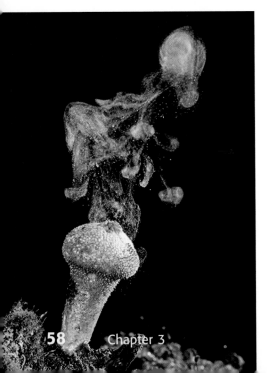

Making More Fungi Reproduction in fungi may be either asexual or sexual. Asexual reproduction occurs in two ways. In one type of asexual reproduction, the hyphae break apart and each new piece becomes a new individual. Asexual reproduction can also occur by the production of spores. **Spores** are small reproductive cells protected by a thick cell wall. Spores are light and easily spread by the wind. See for yourself in **Figure 20**. If the growing conditions where it lands are right, a spore will produce a new fungus.

Sexual reproduction occurs in fungi when special structures form to make sex cells. The sex cells join to produce sexual spores that grow into a new fungus.

Figure 20 *This puffball is releasing spores that can produce new fungi.*

Kinds of Fungi

Fungi are divided into four main groups: threadlike fungi, sac fungi, club fungi, and imperfect fungi. A fungus is classified into a particular group based on its shape and the way it reproduces.

Threadlike Fungi Have you ever seen fuzzy black mold growing on bread? **Molds** are shapeless fuzzy fungi, as shown in **Figure 21.** This particular mold belongs to a group of fungi called *threadlike fungi*. Most of the fungi in this group live in the soil and are usually decomposers, although some are parasites.

Threadlike fungi can reproduce asexually. Extensions of the hyphae grow into the air and form round spore cases at the tips called *sporangia* (spoh RAN jee uh). These sporangia are shown in **Figure 22.** When the sporangia break open, many tiny spores are released into the air.

Threadlike fungi can also reproduce sexually. Two hyphae from different individuals join and develop into specialized sporangia. These sporangia can survive periods of cold or drought. When conditions become more favorable, these specialized sporangia release spores that can grow into new fungi.

Figure 21 *Black bread mold is a soft, cottony mass that grows on bread and fruit.*

Figure 22 *Each of the round sporangia contains thousands of spores.*

Self-Check

What is the relationship between spores and sporangia? *(See page 168 to check your answers.)*

QuickLab

Moldy Bread

If you took a **slice of bread,** moistened it with a few drops of **water,** and then sealed it in a **plastic bag** for 1 week, what do you think would happen? Would the bread get moldy? Why or why not? Where would mold spores come from? How would these spores grow? Design an experiment to check your predictions. How many pieces of bread will you use? Will you treat them the same or differently? Why? If your teacher approves, try your experiment. Did it answer your questions? If not, what changes could you make to get the answers?

Figure 23 *Many people think truffles are delicious. Would you eat them?*

Sac Fungi *Sac fungi* form the largest group of fungi. Sac fungi include yeasts, powdery mildews, truffles, and morels. Truffles are shown in **Figure 23.**

Sexual reproduction in these fungi involves the formation of a sac called an *ascus*. These sacs give the sac fungi their name. Sexually produced spores develop within the ascus. During their life cycles, sac fungi usually reproduce both sexually and asexually.

Most sac fungi are multicellular, but *yeasts* are single-celled sac fungi. Yeasts reproduce asexually by *budding*. In budding, a new cell pinches off from an existing cell. A yeast is budding in **Figure 24.** Yeasts are the only fungi to reproduce by budding.

Figure 24 *Yeasts reproduce by budding. A round scar forms where a bud breaks off of a parent cell. How many times has the larger cell reproduced?*

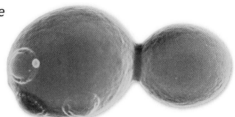

MATH **BREAK**

Multiplying Yeasts

Under ideal conditions, a yeast will produce a new cell by budding in about 30 minutes. Suppose a beaker contains 100 yeast cells. How many cells will it contain after 30 minutes? after 1 hour? after 2 hours? Make a graph to show the increase in size of the yeast population over a period of 5 hours.

Some sac fungi are very useful to humans. One example is yeasts, which are used in making bread. Yeasts use sugar as food and produce carbon dioxide gas and alcohol as waste products. Trapped bubbles of carbon dioxide cause the dough to rise and make bread light and fluffy. Other sac fungi are sources of antibiotics and vitamins. Truffles and morels are prized edible fungi.

Many sac fungi are parasites. They cause plant diseases, such as chestnut blight and Dutch elm disease, shown in **Figure 25.**

Figure 25 *Dutch elm disease is a fungal disease that has killed thousands of elm trees in North America.*

Club Fungi The umbrella-shaped mushrooms are the most commonly known fungi. They belong to a group of fungi called *club fungi.* During sexual reproduction, special hyphae develop and produce clublike structures called *basidia* (buh SID ee uh), the Greek word for "clubs." Sexual spores develop inside the basidia.

What you think of as a mushroom is only the sexual spore-producing part of the organism. The mass of hyphae from which mushrooms are produced may grow 35 m across. Since mushrooms usually grow at the outer edges of the mass of hyphae, they often appear in circles, as shown in **Figure 26.**

The most familiar mushrooms are known as gill fungi because the basidia develop in the grooves, or *gills,* under the cap. Some varieties are grown commercially and sold in supermarkets, but not all gill fungi are edible. The white destroying angel is one type that is very poisonous. Simply a taste of this mushroom can be fatal. See if you can pick out the poisonous fungus in **Figure 27.**

Figure 26 *A ring of mushrooms can appear overnight. In European folk legends, these were known as "fairy rings."*

Figure 27 *Many poisonous mushrooms look good to eat. The mushrooms on the left are edible, but the ones on the right are poisonous.*

A Mushroom Omelet
A friend wants to make a mushroom omelet, but he has no mushrooms. He recently got a mushroom book that has pictures of all the poisonous and edible mushrooms. Using the book, he picks some mushrooms in the woods behind his house. He uses the wild mushrooms to make an omelet. Do you think he should eat the omelet? Why or why not?

Observe a Mushroom

1. Identify the stalk, cap, and gills on a **mushroom** that your teacher has provided.

2. Carefully twist or cut off the cap, and cut it open with a **knife.** Observe the gills with a **magnifying lens.** Look for spores.

3. Observe the other parts of the mushroom with the magnifying lens. The mycelium begins at the bottom of the stalk. Try to find individual hyphae.

4. Sketch the mushroom, and label the parts.

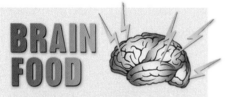

Mushrooms are not the only club fungi. Bracket fungi, puffballs, smuts, and rusts are also in this group of fungi. Bracket fungi grow outward from wood, forming small shelves or brackets, as shown in **Figure 28.** Smuts and rusts are common plant parasites. They often attack crops such as corn and wheat. This can be seen in **Figure 29.**

Figure 28 *Bracket fungi look like shelves on trees. Spores are found on the underside of the bracket.*

Figure 29 *This corn crop is infected with a club fungus called a smut.*

Imperfect Fungi The *imperfect fungi* group includes all the species of fungi that do not quite fit in the other groups. These fungi do not reproduce sexually. Most are parasites that cause diseases in plants and animals. One common human disease caused by these fungi is athlete's foot, a skin disease. Another fungus from this group produces a poison called *aflatoxin,* which can cause cancer.

Some imperfect fungi are useful. *Penicillium,* shown in **Figure 30,** is the source of the antibiotic penicillin. Other imperfect fungi are also used to produce medicines. Some imperfect fungi are used to produce cheeses, soy sauce, and the citric acid used in cola drinks.

BRAIN FOOD

Did you know that stone-washed jeans aren't really washed with stones? They get their faded look from a fungus! Jeans are soaked in a solution containing the fungus *Trichoderma*. This fungus produces enzymes that partially digest the cotton fibers to give jeans a stone-washed appearance.

Figure 30 *The fungus* Penicillium *produces a substance that kills certain bacteria.*

Lichens

A **lichen** is a combination of a fungus and an alga that grow intertwined. The alga actually lives inside the protective walls of the fungus. The resulting organism is different from either of the two organisms growing alone. The merging of the two organisms to form a lichen is so complete that scientists give lichens their own scientific names. **Figure 31** shows examples of lichens.

Unlike fungi, lichens are producers. The algae in the lichens produce food through photosynthesis. Unlike algae, lichens can withstand drying out because of the protective walls of the fungus. Lichens are found in almost every type of terrestrial environment. They can even grow in extreme environments like dry deserts and the Arctic.

Lichens need only air, light, and minerals to grow. This is why lichens can grow on rocks. They produce acids that break down the rock and cause cracks. Bits of rock and dead lichens fill the cracks, making soil that other organisms can grow on.

Lichens absorb water and minerals from the air. As a result, they are easily affected by air pollution. Thus, the presence or absence of lichens is a good measure of air quality in an area.

Jewel lichen

Fruticose lichen

British soldier lichen

Figure 31 *These are some of the many types of lichens.*

SECTION REVIEW

1. How are fungi able to withstand periods of cold or drought?

2. Why are fungi such an important part of the natural world?

3. What are the four main groups of fungi? Give a characteristic of each.

4. **Making Inferences** Why are lichens an example of symbiosis?

internet**connect**

*sci*LINKS
NSTA

TOPIC: Fungi, Lichens
GO TO: www.scilinks.org
*sci*LINKS NUMBER: HSTL265, HSTL270

There's a Fungus Among Us!

Fungi share many characteristics with plants. For example, most fungi live on land. But fungi have several unique features that suggest that they are not closely related to any other kingdom of organisms. In this activity, you will observe some of the unique structures of a mushroom, a member of the kingdom Fungi.

MATERIALS

- mushroom
- tweezers
- 2 sheets of white paper
- masking tape
- Petri dish with fruit-juice agar plate
- incubator
- microscope or magnifying lens
- transparent tape

Procedure

1 Put on your safety goggles and get a mushroom from your teacher. Carefully pull the cap of the mushroom from the stem. Using tweezers, remove a gill from the underside of the cap. Place the gill on a sheet of white paper. Place the mushroom cap gill-side down on the other sheet of paper. Tape the cap in place with masking tape. Place the paper aside for at least 24 hours.

2 Use tweezers to take several 1 cm pieces from the stem, and place them on your agar plate. Record the appearance of the plate in your ScienceLog. Cover the Petri dish and incubate overnight.

3 Use tweezers to gently pull the remaining mushroom stem apart lengthwise. The individual fibers or strings you see are the hyphae that form the structure of the fungus. Place a thin strand on the same piece of paper with the gill you removed from the cap.

4 Observe the gill and the stem hyphae with a magnifying lens or microscope.

5 After at least 24 hours, record in your ScienceLog any changes that occurred on the agar. Carefully lift the mushroom cap from the paper. Place a piece of transparent tape over the print left behind on the paper. Record your observations in your ScienceLog.

Analysis

6 Describe the structures you saw on the gill and hyphae.

7 What is the print on the white paper?

8 Describe the structure at the bottom edge of the mushroom gill. Explain how this structure is connected to the print.

9 Explain how the changes that occurred in your Petri dish are related to methods of fungal reproduction.

Chapter Highlights

Vocabulary

protist *(p. 46)*

funguslike protist *(p. 47)*

parasite *(p. 48)*

host *(p. 48)*

algae *(p. 48)*

phytoplankton *(p. 49)*

protozoa *(p. 52)*

Section Notes

- The protists are a diverse group of single-celled and multicellular organisms. They are grouped in their own kingdom because they differ from other organisms in many ways.

- Funguslike protists are consumers that obtain their food from dead organic matter or from the body of another organism.

- Slime molds and water molds are two groups of funguslike protists.

- Plantlike protists are producers that are also known as algae. Most are aquatic.

- Among the plantlike protists are red algae, brown algae, green algae, diatoms, dinoflagellates, and euglenoids.

- The animal-like protists are single-celled consumers also known as protozoa. Most can move.

- The protozoa include amoebalike protists, flagellates, ciliates, and spore-forming protists.

- Some protists reproduce sexually, some asexually, and some both sexually and asexually.

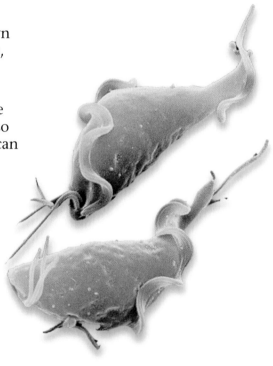

✓ Skills Check

Math Concepts

MICROBE MULTIPLICATION Suppose an amoeba can reproduce by fission once every 30 minutes. If you start with 50 amoebas, after 30 minutes you will have twice as many because each amoeba has divided.

$$2 \times 50 = 100 \text{ amoebas}$$

After 1 hour (30 minutes later) the number of amoebas will double again.

$$2 \times 100 = 200 \text{ amoebas}$$

Visual Understanding

PROTIST STRUCTURE Look at the illustration of *Paramecium* on page 54. Carefully read the labels, and look at each part described. Now do the same thing with the illustration of the euglenoid on page 51. Notice what the two cells have in common and how they differ.

Vocabulary

fungus *(p. 57)*

hyphae *(p. 58)*

mycelium *(p. 58)*

spore *(p. 58)*

mold *(p. 59)*

lichen *(p. 63)*

Section Notes

- Fungi are consumers. They can be decomposers or parasites, or they can live in symbiotic relationships with other organisms.

- Most fungi are made up of chains of cells called hyphae. Many hyphae join together to form a mycelium.

- The four main groups of fungi are threadlike fungi, sac fungi, club fungi, and imperfect fungi.

- Threadlike fungi are primarily decomposers that form sporangia to hold spores.

- Molds are shapeless, fuzzy fungi.

- During sexual reproduction, sac fungi form little sacs in which sexual spores develop.

- Club fungi form structures called basidia during sexual reproduction.

- The imperfect fungi include all the species that do not quite fit anywhere else. Most are parasites that reproduce only by asexual reproduction.

- A lichen is a combination of a specific fungus and a specific alga that is different from either organism growing alone.

internet **connect**

GO TO: go.hrw.com

Visit the **HRW** Web site for a variety of learning tools related to this chapter. Just type in the keyword:

KEYWORD: HSTPRO

GO TO: www.scilinks.org

Visit the **National Science Teachers Association** on-line Web site for Internet resources related to this chapter. Just type in the *sci*LINKS number for more information about the topic:

TOPIC: Algae	*sci*LINKS NUMBER: HSTL255
TOPIC: Protozoa	*sci*LINKS NUMBER: HSTL260
TOPIC: Fungi	*sci*LINKS NUMBER: HSTL265
TOPIC: Lichens	*sci*LINKS NUMBER: HSTL270

Chapter Review

To complete the following sentences, choose the correct term from each pair of terms listed below:

1. Protists that get energy from photosynthesis are ___?___. *(algae* or *amoebas)*

2. *Paramecium* reproduces sexually by ___?___. *(budding* or *conjugation)*

3. The structure containing spores in a sac fungi is called ___?___. *(an ascus* or *a basidium)*

4. ___?___ live on dead organic matter. *(Parasites* or *Decomposers)*

5. Animal-like protists are also called ___?___. *(protozoa* or *algae)*

6. A parasite gets its nutrients from its ___?___. *(host* or *spores)*

UNDERSTANDING CONCEPTS

Multiple Choice

7. Plantlike protists include
   a. euglenoids and ciliates.
   b. lichens and flagellates.
   c. spore-forming protists and smuts.
   d. dinoflagellates and diatoms.

8. Funguslike protists
   a. are consumers or decomposers.
   b. are made of chains of cells called hyphae.
   c. are divided into four major groups.
   d. are always parasites.

9. A euglenoid has
   a. a micronucleus.
   b. pseudopodia.
   c. two flagella.
   d. cilia.

10. Fungi
    a. are producers.
    b. cannot eat or engulf food.
    c. are found only in the soil.
    d. are primarily single-celled.

11. A lichen
    a. is a parasite.
    b. is made up of an alga and a fungus that live intertwined together.
    c. can live only where there is plenty of water.
    d. is a consumer.

12. Animal-like protists
    a. are also known as protozoa.
    b. include amoebas and *Paramecium*.
    c. may be either free living or parasitic.
    d. All of the above

13. A contractile vacuole
    a. is a food passageway.
    b. pumps out excess water.
    c. is the location of food digestion.
    d. can be found in any animal-like protist.

Short Answer

14. How are fungi helpful to humans? How are they harmful?

15. What is the function of cilia in *Paramecium*?

16. What is a red tide?

17. How are slime molds and amoebas similar?

Concept Mapping

18. Use the following terms to create a concept map: fungi, ascus, club fungi, basidia, bread mold, yeast, threadlike fungi, mushrooms.

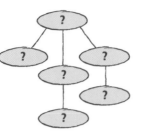

CRITICAL THINKING AND PROBLEM SOLVING

Write one or two sentences to answer the following questions:

19. What might happen if all the protists on Earth died?

20. Water can pass easily through a cell membrane, but too much water can cause a cell to burst. Single-celled amoebas and *Paramecium* have thin cell membranes, and they also live in water. Why don't these organisms burst?

21. You discover some mushrooms in your backyard one morning, and you pull them out of the ground. But the next day you find even more mushrooms. They seem to be growing in a line. Where did the new mushrooms come from?

MATH IN SCIENCE

22. You and your classmates are studying the growth of *Euglena*. Using a microscope, you count the number of organisms in a small container each day. Your teacher says you can expect the number of *Euglena* to double in 1.5 days. If you started out with five *Euglena*, how many *Euglena* do you think you will see on the third day?

INTERPRETING GRAPHICS

Look at the pictures of fungi below, and answer the following questions:

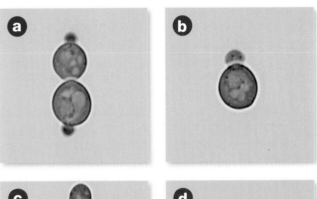

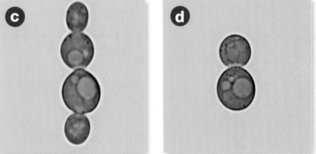

23. What kind of fungus is shown here?

24. What cellular process is shown in these pictures?

25. Which picture was taken first? last? Arrange the pictures in order.

26. Which is the original parent cell? How do you know?

Reading Check-up

Take a minute to review your answers to the Pre-Reading Questions found at the bottom of page 44. Have your answers changed? If necessary, revise your answers based on what you have learned since you began this chapter.

Science, Technology, and Society

Moldy Bandages

When you think of the word *fungus,* you probably think of moldy leftovers in the refrigerator or mushrooms growing at the base of a tree. You may even think of athlete's foot or some other ailment caused by a fungus. Someday you may also think of bandages when you think of fungi. At least that is the hope of Paul Hamlyn and his colleagues at the British Textile Technology Group (BTTG).

▲ *Would you believe that fungi like this may someday be used in surgical bandages?*

Fungi Versus Infection

The scientists at BTTG, along with scientists at the Welsh School of Pharmacy, have discovered that the cell walls of fungi contain polymers that promote the growth of the human cells responsible for rebuilding tissue around a wound. These human healing cells are called fibroblasts, and studies show that the fungal polymers attract and help bind the fibroblasts at a wound. Researchers believe that the polymers react with oxygen to produce hydrogen peroxide. The hydrogen peroxide activates white blood cells and promotes the growth of the fibroblasts. The white blood cells help fight infection around the wound.

From Crab Shells to Wound Healing

Until recently, the only sources of these polymers were crab and prawn shells. The quality and quantity of polymers found in the shells of crabs and prawns vary with weather conditions and with the seasons. Hamlyn's studies have shown that fungi can provide a more consistent product. For even more consistent results, scientists are able to grow fungi in the laboratory in a liquid growth medium.

Where Do We Go from Here?

Although his work is still in the research stage, Hamlyn is working toward a commercial application of the wound-healing fungi. He is researching the possibility of manufacturing two types of bandages from fungi. The first would be made by freeze-drying pieces of the fungi to create an absorbent dressing. This could be used for patients with deep wounds. The second type would be used to help patients with bed sores or diabetic skin ulcers. This bandage would involve a wet dressing of fungi that could be placed over sores or abrasions on the surface of the skin. The fungi would help accelerate the healing process.

Fungi Find the Cure

▶ Fungal products have long been used in the field of medicine. One modern use is cyclosporin. It is a drug used to help prevent the rejection of transplanted organs in humans. Other uses for fungi include a popular folk remedy—placing moldy bread on a wound to promote healing. Research these or other types of medicines that are made from fungi to discover how they work.

It's Alive!

The Maya of Mexico and their descendants believe that Cueva de Villa Luz (the Cave of the Lighted House) is inhabited by powerful spirits. For centuries, they have walked past slimy globs that drip from the cave's ceiling without even thinking about them. When scientists decided to analyze these slime balls, they discovered that the formations are home to billions of microscopic organisms! They nicknamed these colonies "snot-tites" because they resemble mucus.

Life in Battery Acid

As people climb down into the pitch-dark passages of Cueva de Villa Luz, they are greeted by the stench of rotten eggs, an odor rarely found in caves and quickly recognized as potentially deadly hydrogen sulfide gas. This foul and dangerous gas is emitted by the snot-tites! Because it is not safe to remain inside the caverns if there is too much hydrogen sulfide, explorers must constantly monitor the level of the gas in the air.

A closer inspection of snot-tite drippings reveals that they contain sulfuric acid. When sulfuric acid dripped on some of the explorers' clothes, the clothes dissolved right off of their backs!

How do the organisms live in such harsh conditions? It turns out that snot-tites can actually get energy from sulfur, which is toxic to most organisms. And since snot-tites do not have to rely on photosynthesis for energy, they can live in absolute darkness.

A Unique Ecosystem

During dry seasons, the Mayan people feast on tiny fish called mollies that are abundant in the milky-white streams that flow through Cueva de Villa Luz. It's very rare to find so many fish in cave streams. Why are there fish in this cave?

Scientists have discovered that the snot-tites are part of a complex underground ecosystem, possibly unlike any other on Earth. When snot-tites use the sulfur found in the cave, they produce a nutritionally rich waste product. This waste drips into the streams below, where hungry fish can eat it.

Life on Mars?

Many scientists argue that conditions on Mars are too harsh to support any form of life. However, Martian rocks have a large amount of sulfur and scientists know that Mars has caves. Snot-tites have proven that life can exist in these harsh conditions. Someday a space traveler might find a similar organism on Mars!

Going to Extremes

▶ Snot-tites have adapted to extreme environmental conditions that would kill other organisms. Such organisms are called extremophiles. Investigate to find out about other extremophiles. Why are scientists so interested in extremophiles?

◀ *Several billion sulfur-eating microbes can live in a single cubic centimeter of these slimy, gooey snot-tites!*

Introduction to Plants

Sections

1. **What Makes a Plant a Plant?**
   MathBreak 77
   Internet Connect 77

2. **Seedless Plants** 78
   QuickLab 79
   Internet Connect 81

3. **Plants with Seeds** 82
   Environment
   Connection 83
   Apply 83
   Internet Connect 87

4. **The Structures of Seed Plants** 88
   Internet Connect 95

Chapter Lab 96
Chapter Review 100
Feature Articles 102, 103
LabBook 137

Pre-Reading Questions

1. How do plants use flowers and fruits?

2. How are plants different from animals?

GREEN ALIENS?

In Costa Rica's Monteverde cloud forest, a green pattern begins to unfold. It is hidden from all but the most careful observer. It looks alien, but it is very much of this Earth. It is part of a fern, a plant that grows in moist areas. How do we know this patterned mass is a fern? How do we know a fern is a plant? In this chapter, you will learn what plants are, how they differ from one another, and how they survive and reproduce.

These round clusters, called sori, contain structures that produce spores.

OBSERVING PLANT GROWTH

When planting a garden, you bury seeds in the ground, water them, and then wait for tiny sprouts to poke through the soil. What happens to the seeds while they're below the soil? How do seeds grow into plants?

Procedure

1. Fill a **clear 2 L bottle** to within 8 cm of the top with **potting soil.** Your teacher will have already cut off the neck of the bottle.

2. Press **three or four bean seeds** into the soil and against the wall of the bottle. Add an additional 5 cm of potting soil.

3. Cover the sides of the bottle with **aluminum foil** to keep out light. Leave the top uncovered.

4. Water the seeds with about **60 mL of water.** Add more water when the soil dries out.

5. Check on your seeds each day. Record your observations.

Analysis

6. How long did it take for the seeds to germinate?

7. How many seeds grew?

8. Where do the seeds get the energy to start growing?

Introduction to Plants   **73**

Terms to Learn

sporophyte   vascular plant
gametophyte   gymnosperm
nonvascular plant   angiosperm

What You'll Do

◆ Identify the characteristics that all plants share.
◆ Discuss the origin of plants.
◆ Explain how the four main groups of plants differ.

What Makes a Plant a Plant?

Fern

Imagine spending a day without anything made from plants. Not only would it be impossible to make chocolate chip cookies, it would be impossible to do many other things, too. You couldn't wear jeans or any clothes made of cotton or linen. You couldn't use any furniture constructed of wood. You couldn't write with wooden pencils or use paper in any form, including money. You couldn't eat anything because almost all food is made from plants or from animals that eat plants. Spending a day without plants would be very hard to do. In fact, life as we know it would be impossible if plants did not exist!

Sugar maple

Plant Characteristics

Plants come in many different shapes and sizes. What do cactuses, water lilies, ferns, and all other plants have in common? Although one plant may seem very different from another, all plants share certain characteristics.

Plants Make Their Own Food One thing that you have probably noticed about plants is that most of them are green. This is because plant cells have chloroplasts. As you learned earlier, chloroplasts are organelles that contain the green pigment *chlorophyll*. Chlorophyll absorbs light energy from the sun. Plants then use this energy to make food molecules, such as glucose. You may recall that this process is called *photosynthesis*.

Plants Have a Cuticle A *cuticle* is a waxy layer that coats the surface of stems, leaves, and other plant parts exposed to air. Most plants live on dry land, and the cuticle is an adaptation that helps keep plants from drying out.

Prickly pear cactus

Plant Cells Have Cell Walls Plant cells are surrounded by a cell membrane and a rigid cell wall. The cell wall lies outside the cell membrane, as shown in **Figure 1.** The cell wall helps support and protect the plant. Cell walls contain complex carbohydrates and proteins that form a hard material. When the cell reaches its full size, a tough secondary cell wall may develop. Once this wall is formed, a plant cell cannot grow any larger.

Plants Reproduce with Spores and Sex Cells A plant's life cycle can be divided into two parts. Plants spend one part of their lives in the stage that produces spores and the other part in the stage that produces sex cells (egg and sperm cells). The spore-producing stage is called a **sporophyte** (SPOH roh FIET). The stage that produces egg cells and sperm cells is called a **gametophyte** (guh MEET oh FIET). A diagram of the plant life cycle is shown in **Figure 2.**

Spores and sex cells are tiny reproductive cells. Spores that land in a suitable environment, such as damp soil, can grow into new plants. In contrast, sex cells cannot grow directly into new plants. Instead, a male sex cell (sperm cell) must join with a female sex cell (egg cell). The fertilized egg that results may grow into a new plant.

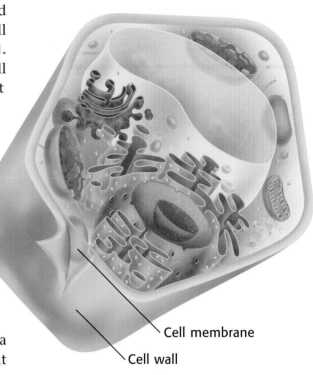

Cell membrane
Cell wall

Figure 1 *In addition to the cell membrane, a cell wall surrounds plant cells.*

Figure 2 Plant Life Cycle

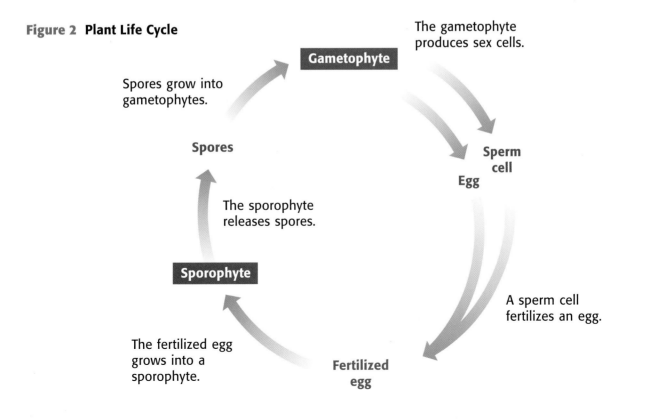

The gametophyte produces sex cells.

Spores grow into gametophytes.

Gametophyte

Spores

Sperm cell

Egg

The sporophyte releases spores.

Sporophyte

A sperm cell fertilizes an egg.

The fertilized egg grows into a sporophyte.

Fertilized egg

The Origin of Plants

If you were to travel back in time 440 million years, Earth would seem like a strange, bare, and unfriendly place. For one thing, no plants lived on land. Where did plants come from?

Take a look at the photographs in **Figure 3**. On the left is an organism called green algae. Plants and green algae are similar in color, but their similarities go beyond color. Green algae and plants contain the same kind of chlorophyll and have similar cell walls. They both store their energy in the form of starch. Like plants, green algae also have a two-part life cycle. These similarities suggest that ancient green algae that lived in the oceans were the ancestors of all plants.

Green algae   Plant

Figure 3 *The similarities between modern green algae and plants suggest that both may have originated from an ancient species of green algae.*

How Are Plants Classified?

There are more than 260,000 species of plants living on Earth today. Although all plants share the basic characteristics discussed earlier, they can be divided into two groups—vascular plants and nonvascular plants.

Plants Without "Plumbing" The nonvascular plants, mosses and liverworts, are shown in **Figure 4**. **Nonvascular plants** have no "pipes" to transport water and nutrients. They depend on diffusion and osmosis to move materials from one part of the plant to another. This is possible because nonvascular plants are small. If they were large—the size of trees, for example—there would be no way to deliver the needed materials to all the cells by diffusion and osmosis.

Moss

Liverwort

Figure 4 *Mosses and liverworts are examples of nonvascular plants.*

✓Self-Check

Green algae cells do not have a cuticle surrounding them. Why do plants need a cuticle, while algae do not? *(See page 168 to check your answer.)*

Plants with "Plumbing" Vascular plants do not rely solely on diffusion and osmosis to deliver needed materials to their cells. **Vascular plants** have tissues that deliver needed materials throughout a plant, much as pipes deliver water to faucets in your home. These tissues are called *vascular tissues*. Because vascular tissues can carry needed materials long distances within the plant body, vascular plants can be almost any size.

Vascular plants can be divided into two groups—plants that produce seeds and plants that do not. Plants that do not produce seeds include ferns, horsetails, and club mosses. Plants that produce seeds also fall into two groups—those that produce flowers and those that do not. Nonflowering plants are called **gymnosperms** (JIM noh SPUHRMZ). Flowering plants are called **angiosperms** (AN jee oh SPUHRMZ). The four main groups of living plants are shown in **Figure 5.**

MATH BREAK

Practice with Percents

The following list gives an estimate of the number of species in each plant group:

Mosses
and liverworts   15,000
Ferns, horsetails,
and club mosses   12,000
Gymnosperms   760
Angiosperms   235,000

What percentage of plants do not produce seeds?

Figure 5 The Main Groups of Living Plants

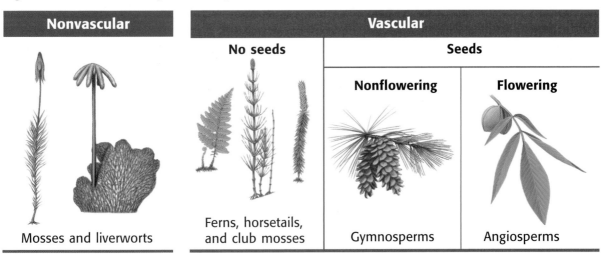

Nonvascular	Vascular		
	No seeds	Seeds	
		Nonflowering	Flowering
Mosses and liverworts	Ferns, horsetails, and club mosses	Gymnosperms	Angiosperms

SECTION REVIEW

1. What are two characteristics that all plants have in common?

2. What type of organism is thought to be the ancestor of all plants? Why?

3. How are ferns, horsetails, and club mosses different from angiosperms?

4. **Applying Concepts** How would you decide whether an unknown organism is a type of green algae or a plant?

internet**connect**

SCLINKS
NSTA

TOPIC: Plant Characteristics,
How Are Plants Classified?
GO TO: www.scilinks.org
*sci*LINKS NUMBER: HSTL280, HSTL285

Terms to Learn

rhizoid
rhizome

What You'll Do

◆ Describe the features of mosses and liverworts.
◆ Describe the features of ferns, horsetails, and club mosses.
◆ Explain how plants without seeds are important to humans and to the environment.

Seedless Plants

Two groups of plants don't make seeds. One group of seedless plants is the nonvascular plants—mosses and liverworts. The other group is made up of several vascular plants—ferns, horsetails, and club mosses.

Mosses and Liverworts

Mosses and liverworts are small. They grow on soil, the bark of trees, and rocks. Because they lack a vascular system, these plants usually live in places that are always wet. Each cell of the plant must absorb water directly from the environment or from a neighboring cell.

Mosses and liverworts don't have true stems, roots, or leaves. They do, however, have structures that carry out the activities of stems, roots, and leaves.

Rock-to-Rock Carpeting Mosses typically live together in large groups, covering soil or rocks with a mat of tiny green plants. Each moss plant has slender, hairlike threads of cells called **rhizoids.** Like roots, rhizoids help hold the plant in place. Each moss plant also has a leafy stalk. The life cycle of the moss alternates between the gametophyte and the sporophyte, as shown in **Figure 6.**

Figure 6 Moss Life Cycle

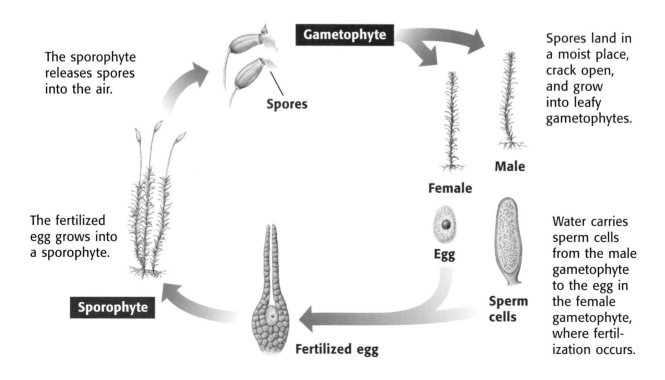

The sporophyte releases spores into the air.

Gametophyte

Spores

Spores land in a moist place, crack open, and grow into leafy gametophytes.

Male

Female

Egg

Water carries sperm cells from the male gametophyte to the egg in the female gametophyte, where fertilization occurs.

Sperm cells

The fertilized egg grows into a sporophyte.

Sporophyte

Fertilized egg

Liverworts Like mosses, liverworts are small, nonvascular plants that usually live in damp or moist places. Liverworts have a life cycle similar to that of mosses. The gametophytes of liverworts can be leafy and mosslike or broad and flattened, like those shown in **Figure 7.** Rhizoids extend out of the lower side of the liverwort body and help anchor the plant.

The Importance of Mosses and Liverworts
Although nonvascular plants are small, they play an important role in the environment. They are usually the first plants to inhabit a new environment, such as newly exposed rock. When the mosses and liverworts die, they form a thin layer of soil in which new plants can grow. New mosses and liverworts cover the soil and help hold it in place. This reduces soil erosion. Mosses also provide nesting materials for birds.

Peat mosses are important to humans. Peat mosses grow in bogs and other wet places. In certain locations, such as Ireland, dead peat mosses have built up thick deposits in bogs. This peat can be taken from the bog, dried, and burned as a fuel.

Figure 7 This liverwort has a broad, flattened gametophyte. The sporophyte looks like a tiny palm tree or umbrella.

Ferns, Horsetails, and Club Mosses

Unlike most of their modern descendants, ancient ferns, horsetails, and club mosses grew to be quite tall. The first forests were made up of 40 m high club mosses, 18 m high horsetails, and 8 m high ferns. **Figure 8** shows how these forests may have looked. These plants had vascular systems and could therefore grow taller than nonvascular plants.

Moss Mass
Determine the mass of a small sample of **dry sphagnum moss.** Place this sample in a **large beaker of water** for 10–15 minutes. What do you think the mass will be after soaking in water? Remove the wet moss from the beaker, and determine its mass. How much mass did the moss gain? Compare your findings with your predictions. What could this absorbent plant be used for? Do some research to find out.

Figure 8 Vascular tissue allowed the ancestors of modern ferns, horsetails, and club mosses to grow tall.

Figure 9 *This fern produces spores in spore cases on the underside of fronds. Fiddleheads grow into new fronds.*

Fiddlehead

Frond

Cluster of
spore cases

Ferns Ferns grow in many places, from the cold Arctic to warm, humid tropical forests. Although most ferns are relatively small plants, some tree ferns in the tropics grow as tall as 23 m.

Figure 9 shows a typical fern. Most ferns have an underground stem, called a **rhizome,** that produces leaves called *fronds* and wiry roots. Young fronds are tightly coiled. They are called *fiddleheads* because they look like the end of a violin, or fiddle.

Like the life cycles of all other plants, the life cycle of ferns, shown in **Figure 10,** is divided into two parts. You are probably most familiar with the sporophyte. The fern gametophyte is a tiny plant about the size of half of one of your fingernails. It is green and flat, and it is usually shaped like a tiny heart. The fern gametophyte has male structures that produce sperm cells and female structures that produce eggs. If a thin film of water is on the ground, the sperm cells can swim through it to an egg.

Figure 10 **Fern Life Cycle**

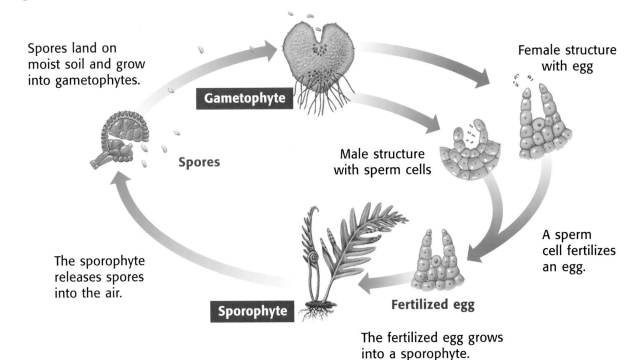

Spores land on moist soil and grow into gametophytes.

Gametophyte

Spores

Female structure with egg

Male structure with sperm cells

A sperm cell fertilizes an egg.

The sporophyte releases spores into the air.

Sporophyte

Fertilized egg

The fertilized egg grows into a sporophyte.

Horsetails Horsetails were common plants millions of years ago, but only about 15 species have survived to the present. Modern horsetails, shown in **Figure 11,** are small vascular plants usually less than 1.3 m tall. They grow in wet, marshy places. Their stems are hollow and contain silica. Because of this, they feel gritty. In fact, pioneers of the early United States called horsetails "scouring rushes" and used them to scrub pots and pans. The life cycle of horsetails is similar to that of ferns.

Club Mosses Club mosses, shown in **Figure 12,** are about 25 cm tall and grow in woodlands. Club mosses are not actually mosses. Unlike true mosses, club mosses have vascular tissue. Like horsetails, club mosses were common plants millions of years ago.

Figure 11 *The conelike tips of horsetails contain spores.*

The Importance of Seedless Vascular Plants Seedless vascular plants play important roles in the environment. Like nonvascular plants, the ferns, horsetails, and club mosses help form soil. They also hold the soil in place, preventing soil erosion.

Ferns are popular as houseplants because of their beautiful leaves. The fiddleheads of some ferns are harvested in early spring, cooked, and eaten.

For humans, some of the most important seedless vascular plants lived and died about 300 million years ago. The remains of these ancient ferns, horsetails, and club mosses formed coal, a fossil fuel that we now extract from the Earth's crust.

Figure 12 *Club mosses release spores from their conelike tips.*

SECTION REVIEW

1. What is the connection between coal and seedless vascular plants?

2. How are horsetails and club mosses similar to ferns?

3. List two ways that seedless vascular plants are important to the environment.

4. **Applying Concepts** Why don't mosses ever grow as large as ferns?

internet**connect**

SCi**LINKS**
NSTA

TOPIC: Seedless Plants
GO TO: www.scilinks.org
*sci*LINKS **NUMBER:** HSTL290

What You'll Do

◆ Compare a seed with a spore.
◆ Describe the features of gymnosperms.
◆ Describe the features of angiosperms.
◆ List the economic and environmental importance of gymnosperms and angiosperms.

Plants with Seeds

Do the plants on this page look familiar to you? They are all seed plants.

As you read earlier, there are two groups of vascular plants that produce seeds—the gymnosperms and the angiosperms. Gymnosperms are trees and shrubs that produce seeds in cones or fleshy structures on stems. Pine, spruce, fir, and ginkgo trees are examples of gymnosperms. Angiosperms, or flowering plants, produce their seeds within a fruit. Peach trees, grasses, oak trees, rose bushes, and buttercups are all examples of angiosperms.

Peaches

Characteristics of Seed Plants

Just like the life cycle of other plants, the life cycle of seed plants alternates between two stages. During part of the cycle, the seed plants are called sporophytes. During another stage, the seed plants are called gametophytes. Gametophytes produce sex cells. But seed plants differ from other plants in the following ways:

English elm

Desert yucca

■ Seed plants produce seeds, structures in which young sporophytes are nourished and protected.

■ Unlike the gametophytes of seedless plants, the gametophytes of seed plants do not live independently of the sporophyte. Gametophytes of seed plants are tiny and are always found protected in the reproductive structures of the sporophyte.

■ The male gametophytes of seed plants do not need water to travel to the female gametophytes. Male gametophytes develop inside tiny structures that can be transported by the wind or by animals. These dustlike structures are called **pollen.**

These characteristics allow seed plants to live just about anywhere. That is why seed plants are the most common plants on Earth today.

What's So Great About Seeds?

A seed develops after fertilization takes place. Fertilization is the union of an egg and a sperm cell. A seed is made up of three parts: a young plant (the sporophyte), stored food, and a tough seed coat that surrounds and protects the young plant. These parts are shown in **Figure 13.**

Figure 13 *A seed contains stored food and a young plant. A seed is surrounded and protected by a seed coat.*

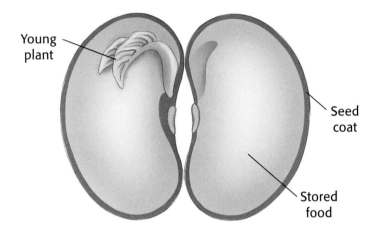

Young plant

Seed coat

Stored food

Plants that reproduce by seeds have several advantages over spore-forming seedless plants. For example, when a seed *germinates,* or begins to grow, the young plant is nourished by the food stored in the seed. By the time the young plant uses up these food reserves, it is able to make all the food it needs by photosynthesis. In contrast, the gametophyte that develops from a spore must be in an environment where it can begin photosynthesis as soon as it begins to grow.

Did you know that seeds like to travel far from home? See how on page 137 of your LabBook.

Environment

C O N N E C T I O N

Animals need plants to live, but some plants need animals, too. These plants produce seeds with tough seed coats that can't begin to grow into new plants until they have been eaten by an animal. When the seed is exposed to the acids and enzymes of the animal's digestive system, the seed coat wears down. After the seed passes out of the animal's digestive tract, it is able to absorb water, germinate, and grow.

 **APPLY**

The Accidental Garden

During the summer, Patrick and his sister love to sit out on the porch munching away on juicy watermelon. One year they held a contest to see who could spit the seeds the farthest. The next spring, Patrick noticed some new plants growing in their yard. When he examined them closely, he realized little watermelons were growing on the plants. Patrick and his sister had no idea that they were starting a watermelon garden. Think about the eating habits of animals in the wild. How might they start a garden?

Introduction to Plants   **83**

Gymnosperms: Seed Plants Without Flowers

The seeds of gymnosperms are not enclosed in a fruit. The word *gymnosperm* is Greek for "naked seed." There are four groups of gymnosperms: conifers, ginkgoes, cycads, and gnetophytes (NEE toh FIETS). Examples are shown in **Figure 14.**

Figure 14 *Gymnosperms do not produce flowers or fruits.*

▲ The **conifers,** with about 550 species, make up the largest group of gymnosperms. Most conifers are evergreen and keep their needle-shaped leaves all year. Conifer seeds develop in cones. Pines, spruces, firs, and hemlocks are examples of conifers.

◀ The **ginkgoes** contain only one living species, the ginkgo tree. Ginkgo seeds are produced in fleshy structures that are attached directly to branches.

▲ The **cycads** were more common millions of years ago. Today there are only about 140 species. These plants grow in the tropics. Like seeds of conifers, seeds of cycads develop in cones.

▲ The **gnetophytes** consist of about 70 species of very unusual plants. This gnetophyte is a shrub that grows in dry areas. Its seeds are formed in cones.

Gymnosperm Life Cycle The gymnosperms that are most familiar to you are probably the conifers. The name *conifer* comes from Greek and Latin words that mean "carry cones." Conifers have two kinds of cones—male and female. These are shown in **Figure 15.** Male spores are produced in the male cones, and female spores are produced in the female cones. The spores develop into gametophytes. The male gametophytes are pollen, dustlike particles that produce sperm cells. The female gametophyte produces eggs. Wind carries pollen from the male cones to the female cones on the same plant or on different plants. The transfer of pollen is called **pollination.**

After the egg is fertilized, it develops into a seed within the female cone. When the seed is mature, it is released by the cone and falls to the ground. The seed then germinates and grows into a new tree. The life cycle of a pine tree is shown in **Figure 16.**

The Importance of Gymnosperms Conifers are the most economically important group of gymnosperms. People harvest conifers and use the wood for building materials and paper products. Pine trees produce a sticky fluid called resin, which is used to make soap, turpentine, paint, and ink.

Figure 15 *A pine tree has male cones and female cones.*

Figure 16 Pine Life Cycle

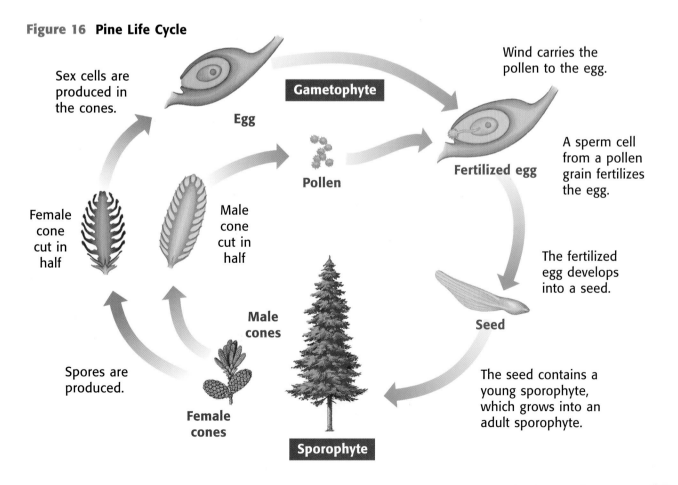

Sex cells are produced in the cones.

Gametophyte

Egg

Pollen

Wind carries the pollen to the egg.

Fertilized egg

A sperm cell from a pollen grain fertilizes the egg.

Female cone cut in half

Male cone cut in half

The fertilized egg develops into a seed.

Seed

Spores are produced.

Male cones

Female cones

The seed contains a young sporophyte, which grows into an adult sporophyte.

Sporophyte

Angiosperms: Seed Plants with Flowers

Flowering plants, or angiosperms, are the most abundant plants today. Angiosperms can be found in almost every environment on land. There are at least 235,000 species of flowering plants, many more than all other plant species combined. Angiosperms come in a wide variety of sizes and shapes, from dandelions and water lilies to prickly-pear cactuses and oak trees.

All angiosperms are vascular plants that produce flowers and fruits. Tulips and roses are examples of flowering plants with large flowers. Other flowering plants, such as grasses and maple trees, have small flowers. After fertilization, angiosperms produce seeds within fruits. Peaches, lemons, and grapes are fruits, as are tomatoes, cucumbers, and many other foods we think of as vegetables.

What Are Flowers For? Flowers help angiosperms reproduce. Some angiosperms depend on the wind for pollination, but others have flowers that attract animals. As shown in **Figure 17,** when animals visit different flowers, they may carry pollen from flower to flower.

What Are Fruits For? Fruits are also important structures for reproduction in angiosperms. They help to ensure that seeds survive as they are transported to areas where new plants can grow. Fruits surround and protect seeds. Some fruits and seeds, such as those shown in **Figure 18,** have structures that help the wind carry them short or long distances. Other fruits may attract animals that eat the fruits and discard the seeds some distance from the parent plant. Prickly burrs are fruits that are carried from place to place by sticking to the fur of animals or to the clothes and shoes of people.

Figure 17 *This bee is on its way to another squash flower, where it will leave some of the pollen it is carrying.*

Figure 18 *Special structures allow some fruits and seeds to float or drift through the air.*

Dandelion

Maple

Milkweed

Monocots and Dicots Angiosperms are divided into two classes—monocots and dicots. The two classes differ in the number of cotyledons in their seeds. A **cotyledon** (KAHT uh LEED uhn) is a seed leaf found inside a seed. Monocot seeds have one cotyledon, and dicot seeds have two cotyledons. Other differences between monocots and dicots are summarized in **Figure 19.** Monocots include grasses, orchids, onions, lilies, and palms. Dicots include roses, cactuses, sunflowers, peanuts, and peas.

The Importance of Angiosperms

Flowering plants provide animals that live on land with the food they need to survive. A deer nibbling on meadow grass is using flowering plants directly as food. An owl that consumes a field mouse is using flowering plants indirectly as food because the field mouse ate seeds and berries.

Humans depend on flowering plants and use them in many ways. All of our major food crops, such as corn, wheat, and rice, are flowering plants. Some flowering plants, such as oak trees, are used to make furniture and toys. Others, such as cotton and flax, supply fibers for clothing and rope. Flowering plants are used to make many medicines as well as cork, rubber, and perfume oils.

Figure 19 Two Classes of Angiosperms

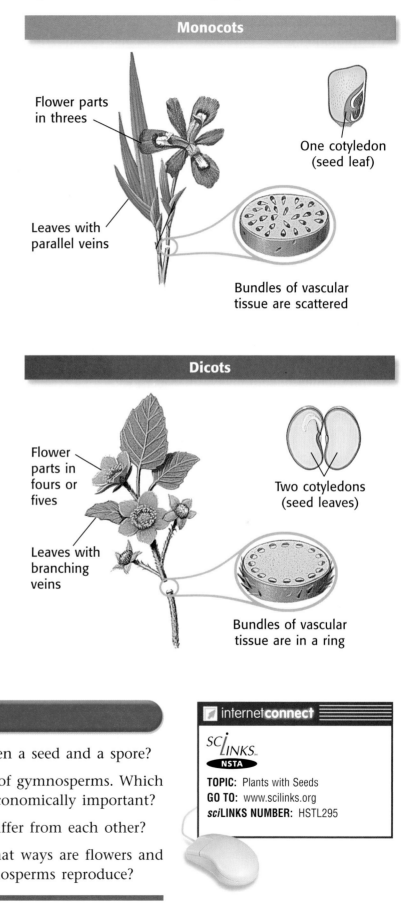

Monocots

Flower parts in threes

Leaves with parallel veins

One cotyledon (seed leaf)

Bundles of vascular tissue are scattered

Dicots

Flower parts in fours or fives

Leaves with branching veins

Two cotyledons (seed leaves)

Bundles of vascular tissue are in a ring

SECTION REVIEW

1. What are two differences between a seed and a spore?

2. Briefly describe the four groups of gymnosperms. Which group is the largest and most economically important?

3. How do monocots and dicots differ from each other?

4. **Identifying Relationships** In what ways are flowers and fruits adaptations that help angiosperms reproduce?

Terms to Learn

xylem	stamen
phloem	pistil
sepal	stigma
petal	ovary

What You'll Do

♦ Describe the functions of roots.
♦ Describe the functions of stems.
♦ Explain how the structure of leaves is related to their function.
♦ Identify the parts of a flower and their functions.

The Structures of Seed Plants

You have different body systems that carry out a variety of functions. For example, your cardiovascular system transports materials throughout your body, and your skeletal system provides support and protection. Similarly, plants have systems too—a root system, a shoot system, and a reproductive system.

Plant Systems

A plant's root system and shoot system supply the plant with needed resources that are found underground and above ground. The root system is made up of roots. The shoot system is made up of stems and leaves.

The root system and the shoot system are dependent on each other. The vascular tissues of the two systems are connected, as shown in **Figure 20.** There are two kinds of vascular tissue—xylem (ZIE luhm) and phloem (FLOH em). **Xylem** transports water and minerals through the plant. **Phloem** transports sugar molecules. Xylem and phloem are found in all parts of vascular plants.

The Root of the Matter

Because most roots are underground, many people do not realize how extensive a plant's root system can be. For example, a 2.5 m tall corn plant can have roots that grow 2.5 m deep and 1.2 m out away from the stem!

Root Functions The main functions of roots are as follows:

- **Roots supply plants with water and dissolved minerals that have been absorbed from the soil.** These materials are transported throughout the plant in the xylem.

- **Roots support and anchor plants.** Roots hold plants securely in the soil.

- **Roots often store surplus food made during photosynthesis.** This food is produced in the leaves and transported as sugar in the phloem to the roots. There the surplus food is usually stored as sugar or starch.

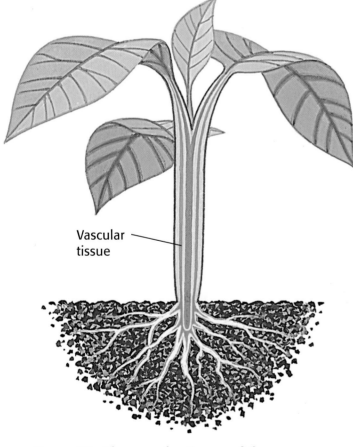

Vascular tissue

Figure 20 *The vascular tissues of the roots and shoots are connected.*

Root Structure The structures of a root are shown in **Figure 21.** Like the cells in the outermost layer of your skin, the layer of cells that covers the surface of roots is called the *epidermis.* Some cells of the root epidermis extend out from the root. These cells, called *root hairs,* increase the amount of surface area through which roots can absorb water and minerals.

After water and minerals are absorbed by the epidermis, they diffuse into the center of the root, where the vascular tissue is located. Roots grow longer at their tips. A group of cells called the *root cap* protects the tip of a root and produces a slimy substance that makes it easier for the root to grow through soil.

Root Types There are two types of roots—taproots and fibrous roots. Examples of each are shown in **Figure 22.**

A *taproot* consists of one main root that grows downward, with many smaller branch roots coming out of it. Taproots can usually obtain water located deep underground. Dicots and gymnosperms have taproots.

A *fibrous root* has several roots of the same size that spread out from the base of the stem. Fibrous roots typically obtain water that is close to the soil surface. Monocots have fibrous roots.

Xylem

Phloem

Growth region

Root cap

Figure 21 *The structures of a root are labeled above.*

Figure 22 *The onion has a fibrous root, and the dandelions and carrots have taproots.*

Fibrous roots

Taproot

Taproots

What's the Holdup?

As shown in **Figure 23,** stems vary greatly in shape and size. Stems are usually located above ground, although many plants have underground stems.

Stem Functions A stem connects a plant's roots to its leaves and flowers and performs these main functions:

- **Stems support the plant body.** Leaves are arranged on stems so that each leaf can absorb the sunlight it needs for photosynthesis. Stems hold up flowers and display them to pollinators.

- **Stems transport materials between the root system and the shoot system.** Xylem carries water and dissolved minerals upward from the roots to the leaves and other shoot parts. Phloem carries the glucose produced during photosynthesis to roots and other parts of the plant.

- **Some stems store materials.** For example, the stems of the plants in **Figure 24** are adapted for water storage.

Valley oak

Figure 23 *The stalks of daisies and the trunks of trees are stems.*

Daisy

BRAIN FOOD

Root or shoot? Even though potatoes grow in the ground, they're not roots. The white potato is an underground stem adapted to store starch.

Figure 24 *Baobab trees store large quantities of water and starch in their massive trunks. Cactuses store water in their thick, green stems.*

Stem Structures

Herbaceous Stems

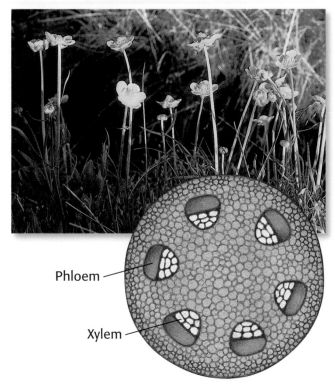

Phloem

Xylem

The plants in this group have stems that are soft, thin, and flexible. These stems are called *herbaceous* stems. Examples of plants with herbaceous (her BAY shuhs) stems include wildflowers, such as clovers and poppies, and many vegetable crops, such as beans, tomatoes, and corn. Some plants with herbaceous stems live only 1 or 2 years. A cross section of one kind of herbaceous stem is shown above.

Woody Stems

Phloem

Xylem

Trees and shrubs have rigid stems made of wood and bark. Their stems are called *woody* stems. If a tree or a shrub lives in an area with cold winters, the plant has a growing period and a dormant period.

At the beginning of each spring growing period, large xylem cells are produced. As fall approaches, the plants produce smaller xylem cells, which appear darker. In the fall and winter, the plants stop producing new cells. The cycle begins again when the spring growing season begins. A ring of dark cells surrounding a ring of light cells make up a growth ring.

SECTION REVIEW

1. What are three functions of roots?

2. What are three functions of stems?

3. **Applying Concepts** Suppose the cross section of a tree reveals 12 light-colored rings and 12 dark-colored rings. How many years of growth are represented?

A Plant's Food Factories

Leaves vary greatly in shape and size. They may be round, narrow, heart-shaped, or fan-shaped. The raffia palm, shown in **Figure 25,** has leaves that may be six times longer than you are tall. A leaf of the duckweed, a tiny aquatic plant also shown in Figure 25, is so small that several can fit on your fingernail.

Sweet gum

Leaf Function The main function of leaves is to make food for the plant. Leaves capture the energy in sunlight and absorb carbon dioxide from the air. Light energy, carbon dioxide, and water are needed to carry out photosynthesis. During photosynthesis, plants use light energy to make food (sugar) from carbon dioxide and water.

Figure 25 *Even though the leaves of these plants are very different, they serve the same purpose.*

Raffia palm

Mimosa

Duckweed

✓Self-Check

How is the function of stems related to the function of leaves? *(See page 168 to check your answers.)*

Leaf Structure The structure of leaves is related to their main function—photosynthesis. **Figure 26** shows a cutaway view of a small block of leaf tissue. The top and bottom surfaces of the leaf are covered with a single layer of cells called the epidermis. Light can easily pass through the thin epidermis to the leaf's interior. Notice the tiny pores in the epidermis. These pores, called *stomata* (singular, *stoma*), allow carbon dioxide to enter the leaf. *Guard cells* open and close the stomata.

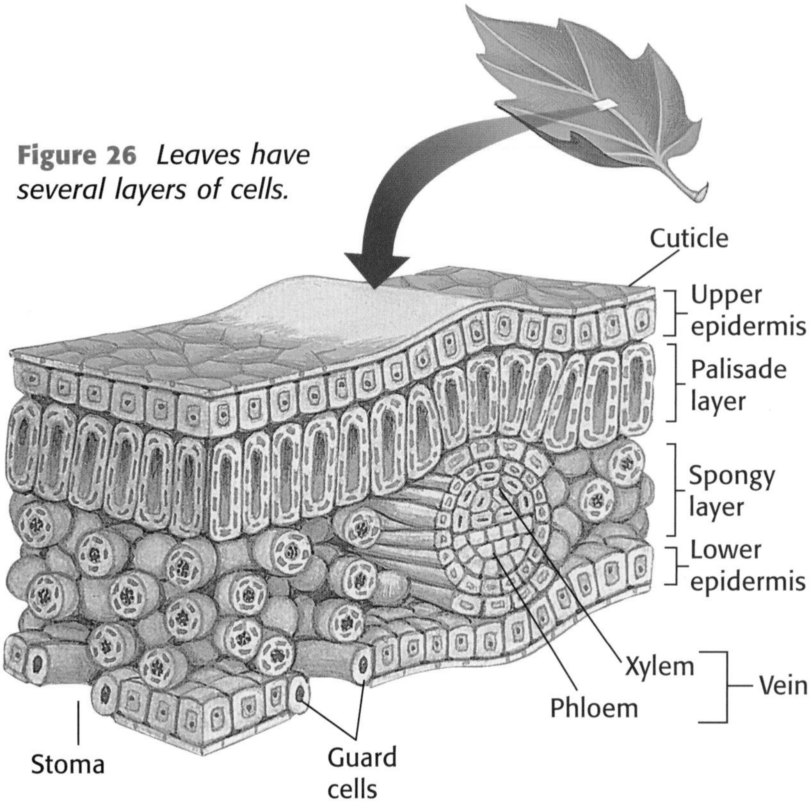

The middle of a leaf, which is where photosynthesis takes place, has two layers. The upper layer is the *palisade layer,* and the lower layer is the *spongy layer.* Cells in the palisade layer contain many chloroplasts, the green organelles that carry out photosynthesis. Cells in the spongy layer are spread farther apart than cells in the palisade layer. The air spaces between these cells allow carbon dioxide to diffuse more freely throughout the leaf.

The veins of a leaf contain xylem and phloem surrounded by supporting tissue. Xylem transports water and minerals to the leaf. Phloem conducts the sugar made during photosynthesis from the leaf to the rest of the plant.

Leaf Adaptations Some leaves have functions other than photosynthesis. For example, the leaves on a cactus plant are modified as spines. These hard, pointed leaves discourage animals from eating the succulent cactus stem. **Figure 27** shows leaves with a most unusual function. The leaves of a sundew are modified to catch insects. Sundews grow in soil that does not contain enough nitrogen to meet the plants' needs. By catching and digesting insects, a sundew is able to meet its nitrogen requirement.

Figure 26 *Leaves have several layers of cells.*

Cuticle
Upper epidermis
Palisade layer
Spongy layer
Lower epidermis
Xylem
Phloem
Vein
Stoma
Guard cells

Figure 27 *This damselfly is trapped in the sticky fluid of a sundew flower.*

Flowers

Most people admire the beauty of flowers, such as roses or lilies, without stopping to think about *why* plants have flowers. Flowers are adaptations for sexual reproduction. Flowers come in many different shapes, colors, and fragrances that attract pollinators or catch the wind. Flowers usually contain the following parts: sepals, petals, stamens, and one or more pistils. The flower parts are usually arranged in rings around the central pistil. **Figure 28** shows the parts of a typical flower.

Orchid

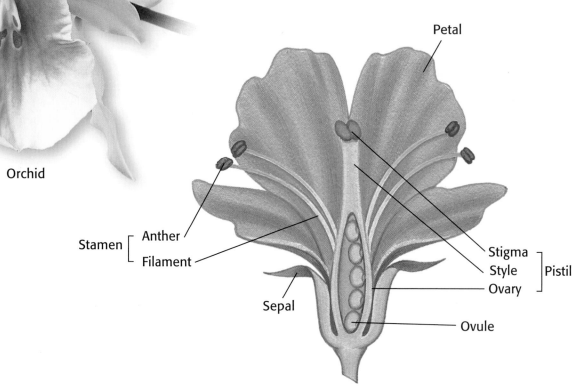

Figure 28 *The stamens, which produce pollen, and the pistil, which produces eggs, are surrounded by the petals and the sepals.*

Sepals make up the bottom ring of flower parts. They are often green like leaves. The main function of sepals is to cover and protect the immature flower when it is a bud. As the blossom opens, the sepals fold back so that the petals can enlarge and become visible.

Petals are broad, flat, and thin, like sepals, but they vary in shape and color. Petals may attract insects or other animals to the flower. These animals help plants reproduce by transferring pollen from flower to flower.

Just above the petals is a circle of **stamens,** which are the male reproductive structures. Each stamen consists of a thin stalk called a *filament,* and each stamen is topped by an *anther.* Anthers are saclike structures that produce pollen grains.

In the center of most flowers is one or more **pistils,** the female reproductive structures. The tip of the pistil is called the **stigma.** Pollen grains collect on stigmas, which are often sticky or feathery. The long, slender part of the pistil is the *style.* The rounded base of the pistil is called the **ovary.** As shown in **Figure 29,** the ovary contains one or more *ovules.* Each ovule contains an egg. If fertilization occurs, the ovule develops into a seed, and the ovary develops into a fruit.

Flowers that have brightly colored petals and aromas usually depend on animals for pollination. Plants without bright colors and aromas, such as the grass flowers shown in **Figure 30,** depend on wind to spread pollen.

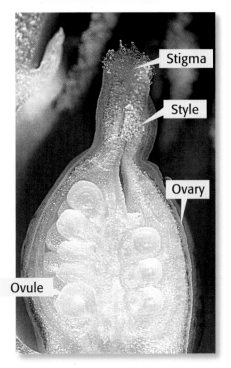

Figure 29 *This hyacinth ovary contains many ovules.*

Figure 30 *The tall stems of these pampas grass flowers allow their pollen to be picked up by the wind.*

SECTION REVIEW

1. Describe the internal structure of a typical leaf. How is a leaf's structure related to its function?

2. Which flower structure produces pollen?

3. **Identifying Relationships** Compare the functions of xylem and phloem in roots, stems, leaves, and flowers.

internet**connect**

SCI*LINKS*
NSTA

TOPIC: The Structure of Seed Plants
GO TO: www.scilinks.org
*sci***LINKS NUMBER:** HSTL300

Leaf Me Alone!

Imagine you are a naturalist all alone on an expedition in a rain forest. You have found several plants that you think have never been seen before. You must contact a botanist, a scientist who studies plants, to confirm your suspicion. Because there is no mail service in the rain forest, you must describe these species completely and accurately by radio. The botanist must be able to draw the leaves of the plants from your description.

In this activity, you will carefully describe five plant specimens using the examples and vocabulary lists in this lab.

MATERIALS

- 5 different leaf specimens
- plant guidebook (optional)

Procedure

1. Examine the leaf characteristics illustrated in this lab. These examples can be found on the following page. You will notice that more than one term is needed to completely describe a leaf.

2. In your ScienceLog, draw a diagram of a leaf from each plant specimen.

3. Next to each drawing, carefully describe the leaf. Include general characteristics, such as relative size and color. For each plant, identify the following: leaf shape, stem type, leaf arrangement, leaf edge, vein arrangement, and leaf-base shape. Use the terms and vocabulary lists provided on the next page to describe each leaf as accurately as possible and to label your drawings.

Analysis

4. What is the difference between a simple leaf and a compound leaf?

5. Describe two different vein arrangements in leaves.

6. Based on what you know about adaptation, explain why there are so many different leaf variations.

Going Further

Choose a partner. Using the keys and vocabulary in this lab, describe a leaf, and see if your partner can draw the leaf from your description. Switch roles and see if you can draw a leaf from your partner's description.

Leaf Shapes Vocabulary List

cordate—heart shaped

lanceolate—sword shaped

lobate—lobed

oblong—leaves rounded at the tip

orbicular—disk shaped

ovate—oval shaped, widest at base of leaf

peltate—shield shaped

reniform—kidney shaped

sagittate—arrow shaped

Stems Vocabulary List

woody—bark or barklike covering on stem

herbaceous—green, nonwoody stems

Leaf Arrangements Vocabulary List

alternate—alternating leaves or leaflets along stem or petiole

compound—leaf divided into segments or several leaflets on a petiole

opposite—compound leaf with several leaflets arranged oppositely along a petiole

palmate—single leaf with veins arranged around a center point

palmate compound—several leaflets arranged around a center point

petiole—leaf stalk

pinnate—single leaf with veins arranged along a center vein

pinnate compound—several leaflets on either side of a petiole

simple—single leaf attached to stem by a petiole

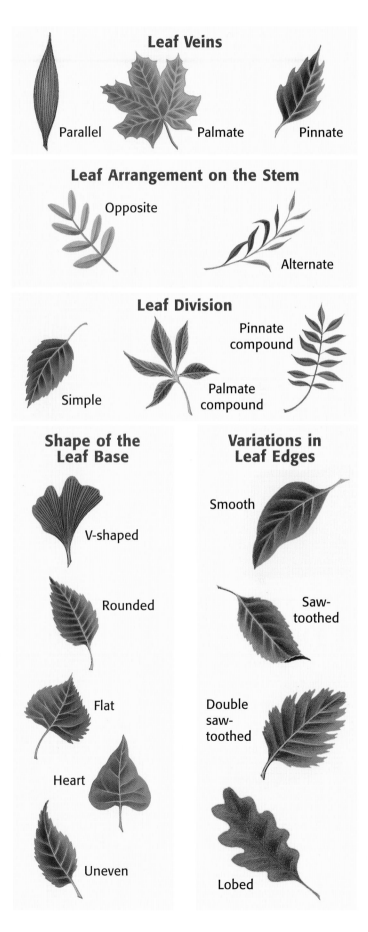

Leaf Veins

Parallel   Palmate   Pinnate

Leaf Arrangement on the Stem

Opposite

Alternate

Leaf Division

Pinnate compound

Simple   Palmate compound

Shape of the Leaf Base

V-shaped

Rounded

Flat

Heart

Uneven

Variations in Leaf Edges

Smooth

Saw-toothed

Double saw-toothed

Lobed

Chapter Highlights

SECTION 1

Vocabulary

sporophyte *(p. 75)*

gametophyte *(p. 75)*

nonvascular plant *(p. 76)*

vascular plant *(p. 77)*

gymnosperm *(p. 77)*

angiosperm *(p. 77)*

Section Notes

• Plants use photosynthesis to make food. Plant cells have cell walls. Plants are covered by a waxy cuticle.

• The life cycle of a plant includes a spore-producing stage (the sporophyte) and a sex-cell-producing stage (the gametophyte).

• Plants probably evolved from a type of ancient green algae.

• Vascular plants have tissues that carry materials throughout a plant. Nonvascular plants do not have vascular tissues and must depend on diffusion and osmosis to move materials.

SECTION 2

Vocabulary

rhizoid *(p. 78)*

rhizome *(p. 80)*

Section Notes

• There are two groups of plants that do not make seeds.

• Mosses and liverworts are small, nonvascular plants. They are small because they lack xylem and phloem. Mosses and liverworts need water to transport sperm cells to eggs.

• Ferns, horsetails, and club mosses are vascular plants. They can grow larger than nonvascular plants. Ferns, horsetails, and club mosses need water to transport sperm cells to eggs.

☑ Skills Check

Math Concepts

DO THE PERCENTAGES ADD UP? If 38 percent of the plants in a forest are flowering plants, what percentage of the plants are not flowering plants? The two groups together make up 100 percent. So subtract 38 percent from 100.

100 percent – 38 percent = 62 percent

Look again at the MathBreak on page 77. You can calculate the percentage of plants that do produce seeds by subtracting your MathBreak answer from 100 percent.

Visual Understanding

SEEDS This image shows the two cotyledons of a dicot seed. The seed has been split, and the two cotyledons laid open like two halves of a hamburger bun. You are looking at the inside surfaces of the two cotyledons. Open a peanut and see for yourself. In peanuts, the two cotyledons come apart very easily. You can even see the young delicate plant inside.

SECTION 3

Vocabulary

pollen *(p. 82)*

pollination *(p. 85)*

cotyledon *(p. 87)*

Section Notes

- Seed plants are vascular plants that produce seeds. The sperm cells of seed plants develop inside pollen.

- Gymnosperms are seed plants that produce their seeds in cones or in fleshy structures attached to branches. The four groups of gymnosperms are conifers, ginkgoes, cycads, and gnetophytes.

- Angiosperms are seed plants that produce their seeds in flowers. The two groups of flowering plants are monocots and dicots.

Labs

Travelin' Seeds *(p. 137)*

SECTION 4

Vocabulary

xylem *(p. 88)*

phloem *(p. 88)*

sepal *(p. 94)*

petal *(p. 94)*

stamen *(p. 95)*

pistil *(p. 95)*

stigma *(p. 95)*

ovary *(p. 95)*

Section Notes

- Roots generally grow underground. Roots anchor the plant, absorb water and minerals, and store food.

- Stems connect roots and leaves. Stems support leaves and other structures; transport water, minerals, and food; and store water and food.

- The main function of leaves is photosynthesis. Leaf structure is related to this function.

- Flowers usually have four parts—sepals, petals, stamens, and pistils. Stamens produce sperm cells in pollen. The ovary in the pistil contains ovules. Each ovule contains an egg. Ovules become seeds after fertilization.

 internet connect

GO TO: go.hrw.com

Visit the **HRW** Web site for a variety of learning tools related to this chapter. Just type in the keyword:

KEYWORD: HSTPL1

GO TO: www.scilinks.org

Visit the **National Science Teachers Association** on-line Web site for Internet resources related to this chapter. Just type in the *sci*LINKS number for more information about the topic:

TOPIC: Plant Characteristics	*sci*LINKS NUMBER: HSTL280
TOPIC: How Are Plants Classified?	*sci*LINKS NUMBER: HSTL285
TOPIC: Seedless Plants	*sci*LINKS NUMBER: HSTL290
TOPIC: Plants with Seeds	*sci*LINKS NUMBER: HSTL295
TOPIC: The Structure of Seed Plants	*sci*LINKS NUMBER: HSTL300

Chapter Review

To complete the following sentences, choose the correct term from each pair of terms listed below:

1. The __?__ is a waxy layer that coats the surface of stems and leaves. *(stomata* or *cuticle)*

2. During the plant life cycle, eggs and sperm cells are produced by the __?__. *(sporophyte* or *gametophyte)*

3. In vascular plants, __?__ transports water and minerals, and __?__ transports food molecules, such as sugar. *(xylem/phloem* or *phloem/xylem)*

4. Seedless vascular plants include ferns, horsetails, and __?__. *(club mosses* or *liverworts)*

5. A __?__ is a seed leaf found inside a seed. *(cotyledon* or *sepal)*

6. In a flower, the __?__ are the male reproductive structures. *(pistils* or *stamens)*

UNDERSTANDING CONCEPTS

Multiple Choice

7. Which of the following plants is nonvascular?
   a. fern
   b. moss
   c. conifer
   d. monocot

8. Coal formed millions of years ago from the remains of
   a. nonvascular plants.
   b. flowering plants.
   c. green algae.
   d. seedless vascular plants.

9. The largest group of gymnosperms is the
   a. conifers.
   b. ginkgoes.
   c. cycads.
   d. gnetophytes.

10. Roots
    a. absorb water and minerals.
    b. store surplus food.
    c. anchor the plant.
    d. All of the above

11. Woody stems
    a. are soft, green, and flexible.
    b. include the stems of daisies.
    c. contain wood and bark.
    d. All of the above

12. The veins of a leaf contain
    a. xylem and phloem.
    b. stomata.
    c. epidermis and cuticle.
    d. xylem only.

13. In a flower, petals function to
    a. produce ovules.
    b. attract pollinators.
    c. protect the flower bud.
    d. produce pollen.

14. Monocots have
    a. flower parts in fours or fives.
    b. two cotyledons in the seed.
    c. parallel veins in leaves.
    d. All of the above

Short Answer

15. What advantages does a seed have over a spore?

16. How is water important to the reproduction of mosses and ferns?

Concept Map

17. Use the following terms to create a concept map: nonvascular plants, vascular plants, xylem, phloem, ferns, seeds in cones, plants, gymnosperms, spores, angiosperms, seeds in flowers.

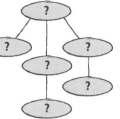

CRITICAL THINKING AND PROBLEM SOLVING

Write one or two sentences to answer the following questions:

18. Plants that are pollinated by wind produce much more pollen than plants that are pollinated by animals. Why do you suppose this is so?

19. If plants did not possess a cuticle, where would they have to live? Why?

20. Grasses do not have strong aromas or bright colors. How might this be related to the way these plants are pollinated?

21. Imagine that a seed and a spore are beginning to grow in a deep, dark crack in a rock. Which reproductive structure—the seed or the spore—is more likely to survive and develop into an adult plant after it begins to grow? Explain your answer.

MATH IN SCIENCE

22. One year a maple tree produced 1,056 seeds. If only 15 percent of those seeds germinated and grew into seedlings, how many seedlings would there be?

INTERPRETING GRAPHICS

23. Examine the cross section of the flower below to answer the following questions:
   a. Which letter corresponds to the structure in which pollen is produced? What is the name of this structure?
   b. Which letter corresponds to the structure that contains ovules? What is the name of this structure?

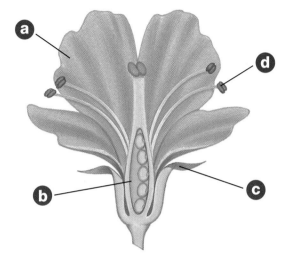

24. In a woody stem, a ring of dark cells and a ring of light cells represent 1 year of growth. Examine the cross section of a tree trunk below, and determine the age of the tree.

Reading Check-up

Take a minute to review your answers to the Pre-Reading Questions found at the bottom of page 72. Have your answers changed? If necessary, revise your answers based on what you have learned since you began this chapter.

Science, Technology, and Society

Supersquash or Frankenfruit?

The fruits and vegetables you buy at the supermarket may not be exactly what they seem. Scientists may have genetically altered these foods to make them look and taste better, contain more nutrients, or have a longer shelf life.

From Bullets to Bacteria

Through genetic engineering, scientists are now able to duplicate one organism's DNA and place a certain gene from the DNA into the cells of another species of plant or animal. This technology enables scientists to give plants and animals a new trait. The new trait can then be passed along to the organism's offspring and future generations.

Scientists alter plants by inserting a gene with a certain property into a plant's cells. The DNA is usually inserted by one of two methods. In one method, new DNA is first placed inside a special bacterium, and the bacterium carries the DNA into the plant cell. In another method, microscopic particles of metal coated with the new DNA are fired into the plant cells with a special "gene gun."

High-tech Food

During the past decade, scientists have inserted genes into more than 50 different kinds of plants. In most cases, the new trait from the inserted gene makes the plants more disease resistant or more marketable in some way. For example, scientists have added genes from a caterpillar-attacking bacterium to cotton, tomato, and potato plants. The altered plants produce proteins that kill the crop-eating caterpillars. Scientists are also trying to develop genetically altered peas and red peppers that stay sweeter longer. A genetically altered tomato that lasts longer and tastes better is already in many supermarkets. One day it may even be possible to create a caffeine-free coffee bean.

Are We Ready?

As promising as these genetically engineered foods seem to be, they are not without controversy. Some scientists are afraid that genes introduced to crop plants could be released into the environment or that foods may be changed in ways that endanger human health. For example, could people who are allergic to peanuts become sick from eating a tomato plant that contains certain peanut genes? All of these concerns will have to be addressed before the genetically altered food products are widely accepted.

Find Out for Yourself

▶ Are genetically altered foods controversial in your area? Survey a few people to get their opinions about genetically altered foods. Do they think grocery stores should carry these foods? Why or why not?

◀ *A scientist uses a "gene gun" to insert DNA into plant cells.*

CAREERS

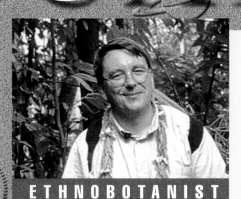

ETHNOBOTANIST

Paul Cox is an *ethnobotanist.* He travels to remote places to look for plants that can help cure diseases. He seeks the advice of shamans and other native healers in his search. In 1984, Cox made a trip to Samoa to observe healers. While there he met a 78-year-old Samoan healer named Epenesa. She was able to identify more than 200 medicinal plants, and she astounded Cox with her knowledge. Epenesa had an accurate understanding of human anatomy, and she dispensed medicines with great care and accuracy.

*I*n Samoan culture, the healer is one of the most valued members of the community. After all, the healer has the knowledge to treat diseases. In some cases, Samoan healers know about ancient treatments that Western medicine has yet to discover. Recently, some researchers have turned to Samoan healers to ask them about their medical secrets.

Blending Polynesian and Western Medicine

After Cox spent months observing Epenesa as she treated patients, Epenesa gave him her treatment for yellow fever—a tea made from the wood of a rain-forest tree. Cox brought the yellow-fever remedy to the United States, and in 1986 researchers at the National Cancer Institute (NCI) began studying the plant. They found that the plant contains a virus-fighting chemical called *prostratin.* Further research by NCI indicates that prostratin may also have potential as a treatment for AIDS.

Another compound from Samoan healers treats inflammation. The healers apply the bark of a local tree to the inflamed skin. When a team of scientists evaluated the bark, they found that the healers were absolutely correct. The active compound in the bark, *flavanone,* is now being researched for its medicinal properties. Some day Western doctors may prescribe medicine containing flavanone.

Preserving Their Knowledge

When two of the healers Cox observed in Samoa died in 1993, generations of medical knowledge died with them. The healers' deaths point out the urgency of recording the ancient wisdom before all of the healers are gone. Cox and other ethnobotanists must work hard to gather information from healers as quickly as they can.

The Feel of Natural Healing

▶ The next time you have a mosquito bite or a mild sunburn, consider a treatment that comes from the experience of Native American healers. Aloe vera, another plant product, is found in a variety of lotions and ointments. Find out how well it works for you!

▶ *These plant parts from Samoa may one day be used in medicines to treat a variety of diseases.*

Plant Processes

Sections

(1) **The Reproduction of
Flowering Plants.....** 106
  QuickLab 108
  Internet Connect 109

(2) **The Ins and Outs of
Making Food........** 110
  Internet Connect 112

(3) **Plant Responses to
the Environment.....** 113
  MathBreak 113
  QuickLab 114
  Astronomy
    Connection 115
  Apply 116
  Internet Connect 117

Chapter Lab 118

Chapter Review 122

Feature Articles...... 124, 125

LabBook 138–139

Pre-Reading
Questions

1. How do plants respond
   to changes in their
   environment?

2. Why do plants need
   light?

VENUS'S-FLYTRAP

Look at the plant in the photo. Yes, those green spiny pads
are its leaves. Why is the Venus's-flytrap such an unusual
plant? Unlike most plants, the Venus's-flytrap eats meat. It
obtains key nutrients by capturing and digesting insects
and other small animals. The two green pads snap shut to
trap the prey. In this chapter, you will learn how different
types of plants reproduce themselves, respond to their
environments, and take in nutrients. You will also learn
how plants use sunlight to create food.

WHICH END IS UP?

If you plant seeds with their "tops" facing in different directions, will their stems all grow upward? Do this activity to find out.

Procedure

1. Pack a **clear medium plastic cup** with slightly **moistened paper towels.**

2. Place **5 or 6 corn seeds,** equally spaced, around the cup between the cup and the paper towels. Point the tip of each seed in a different direction.

3. Use a **marker** to draw arrows on the outside of the cup to indicate the direction that each seed tip points.

4. Place the cup in a well-lit location for one week. Keep the seeds moist by adding **water** to the paper towels as needed.

5. After one week, observe the plant growth. Record the direction in which each plant grew.

Analysis

6. Compare the direction of growth for your seeds. What explanation can you give for the results?

What You'll Do

- Describe the roles of pollination and fertilization in sexual reproduction.
- Describe how fruits are formed from flowers.
- Explain the difference between sexual and asexual reproduction in plants.

The Reproduction of Flowering Plants

If you went outside right now and made a list of all the different kinds of plants you could see, most of the plants on your list would probably be flowering plants. Flowering plants are the largest and the most diverse group of plants in the world. Their success is partly due to their flowers, which are adaptations for sexual reproduction. During sexual reproduction, an egg is fertilized by a sperm cell. In flowering plants, fertilization takes place within the flower and leads to the formation of one or more seeds within a fruit.

How Does Fertilization Occur?

In order for fertilization to occur, sperm cells must be able to reach eggs. The sperm cells of a flowering plant are contained in pollen grains. Pollination occurs when pollen grains are transported from anthers to stigmas. This is the beginning of fertilization, as shown in **Figure 1.** After the pollen lands on the stigma, a tube grows from the pollen grain through the style to the ovary. Inside the ovary are ovules. Each ovule contains an egg.

Sperm cells within the pollen grain move down the pollen tube and into an ovule. Fertilization occurs as one of the sperm cells fuses with the egg inside the ovule.

Figure 1 *Fertilization occurs after pollination.*

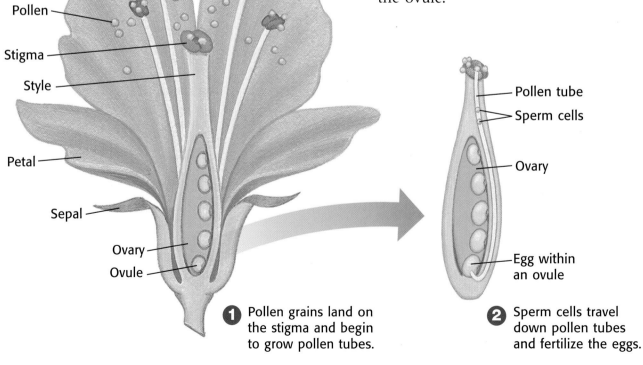

Anther
Pollen
Stigma
Style
Petal
Sepal
Ovary
Ovule

Pollen tube
Sperm cells
Ovary
Egg within an ovule

❶ Pollen grains land on the stigma and begin to grow pollen tubes.

❷ Sperm cells travel down pollen tubes and fertilize the eggs.

From Flower to Fruit

After fertilization takes place, the ovule develops into a seed that contains a tiny, undeveloped plant. The ovary surrounding the ovule develops into a fruit. **Figure 2** shows how the ovary and ovules of a flower develop into a fruit and seeds.

Figure 2 *Fertilization leads to the development of fruit and seeds.*

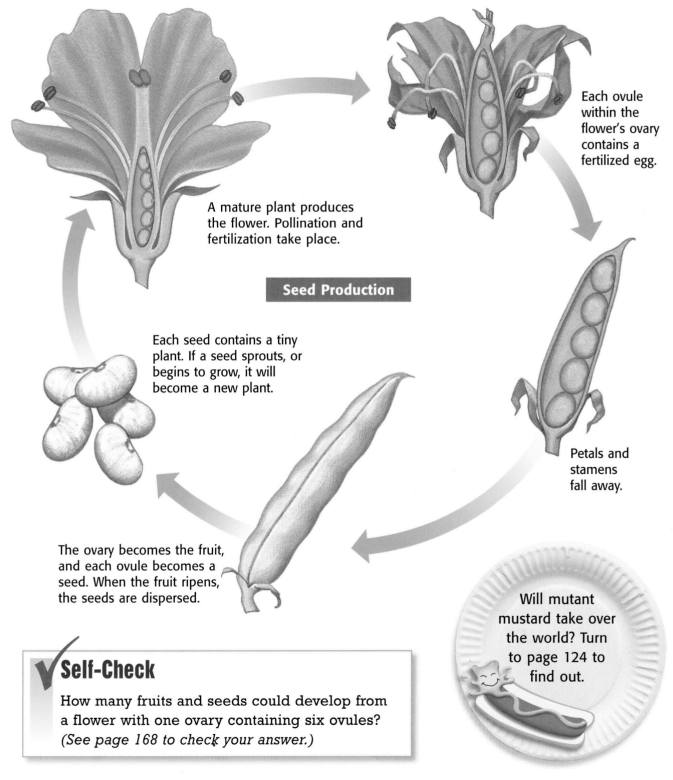

Seed Production

A mature plant produces the flower. Pollination and fertilization take place.

Each ovule within the flower's ovary contains a fertilized egg.

Petals and stamens fall away.

The ovary becomes the fruit, and each ovule becomes a seed. When the fruit ripens, the seeds are dispersed.

Each seed contains a tiny plant. If a seed sprouts, or begins to grow, it will become a new plant.

✔ Self-Check

How many fruits and seeds could develop from a flower with one ovary containing six ovules? *(See page 168 to check your answer.)*

Will mutant mustard take over the world? Turn to page 124 to find out.

Familiar Fruits

While the ovules are developing into seeds, the ovary is developing into the fruit. As the fruit swells and ripens, it holds and protects the developing seeds. Look below to see which parts of the fruits developed from a flower's ovary and ovules.

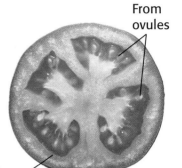

From ovules

From ovary

Tomato

From ovary

From ovules

Orange

From ovary

From ovule

Avocado

Thirsty Seeds

1. Obtain **12 dry bean seeds, 2 Petri dishes,** a **wax pencil,** and **water** from your teacher.

2. Fill one Petri dish two-thirds full of water and add six seeds. Label the dish "Water."

3. Add the remaining seeds to the dry Petri dish. Label this dish "Control."

4. The next day, compare the size of the two sets of seeds. Write your observations in your ScienceLog.

5. What caused the size of the seeds to change? Why might this be important to the seed's survival?

Seeds Become New Plants

Once a seed is fully developed, the young plant inside the seed stops growing. The seed may become dormant. When seeds are **dormant,** they are inactive. Dormant seeds can often survive long periods of drought or freezing temperatures. Some seeds need extreme conditions such as cold winters or even forest fires to break their dormancy.

When a seed is dropped or planted in an environment that has water, oxygen, and a suitable temperature, the seed sprouts. Each plant species has an ideal temperature at which most of its seeds will begin to grow. For most plants, the ideal temperature for growth is about 27°C (80.6°F). **Figure 3** shows the *germination,* or sprouting, of a bean seed and the early stages of growth in a young bean plant.

Figure 3 *Sexual reproduction produces seeds that grow into new plants.*

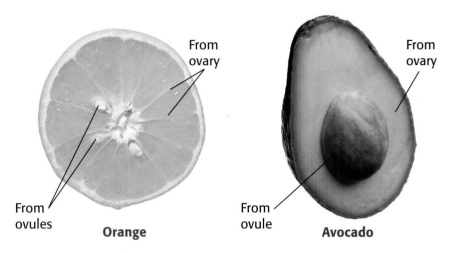

Other Methods of Reproduction

Many flowering plants can also reproduce asexually. Asexual reproduction in plants does not involve the formation of flowers, seeds, and fruits. In asexual reproduction, a part of a plant, such as a stem or root, produces a new plant. Several examples of asexual reproduction are shown below in **Figure 4**.

Figure 4 *Asexual reproduction can occur in several different ways. Some examples are shown here.*

▼ The strawberry plant produces runners, stems that run horizontally along the ground. Buds along runners grow into new plants.

▲ The "eyes" of potatoes are buds that can grow asexually into new plants.

Kalanchoe plants produce plantlets, ▶ tiny plants along the margins of their leaves. Plantlets eventually fall off and root in the soil as separate plants.

SECTION REVIEW

1. How does pollination differ from fertilization?

2. Which part of a flower develops into a fruit?

3. **Relating Concepts** What do flowers and runners have in common? How are they different?

4. **Identifying Relationships** When might asexual reproduction be important for the survival of some flowering plants?

internet**connect**

SC*i*LINKS.
NSTA

TOPIC: Reproduction of Plants
GO TO: www.scilinks.org
*sci***LINKS NUMBER:** HSTL305

Terms to Learn

chlorophyll
cellular respiration
stomata
transpiration

What You'll Do

◆ Describe the process of
  photosynthesis.
◆ Discuss the relationship
  between photosynthesis
  and cellular respiration.
◆ Explain the importance of
  stomata in the processes
  of photosynthesis and
  transpiration.

The Ins and Outs of Making Food

Plants do not have lungs, but they need air just like you. Air is a mixture of oxygen, carbon dioxide, and other gases. Plants must have carbon dioxide to carry out photosynthesis, which is how they make their own food.

What Happens During Photosynthesis?

Plants need sunlight to produce food. During photosynthesis, the energy in sunlight is used to make food in the form of the sugar glucose ($C_6H_{12}O_6$) from carbon dioxide (CO_2) and water (H_2O). How does this happen?

Capturing Light Energy Plant cells have organelles called chloroplasts. Chloroplasts contain **chlorophyll,** a green pigment that absorbs light energy. You may not know it, but sunlight is actually a mixture of all the colors of the rainbow. **Figure 5** shows how light from the sun can be separated into different colors when passed through a triangular piece of glass called a prism. Chlorophyll absorbs all of the colors in light except green. Plants look green because chlorophyll reflects green light.

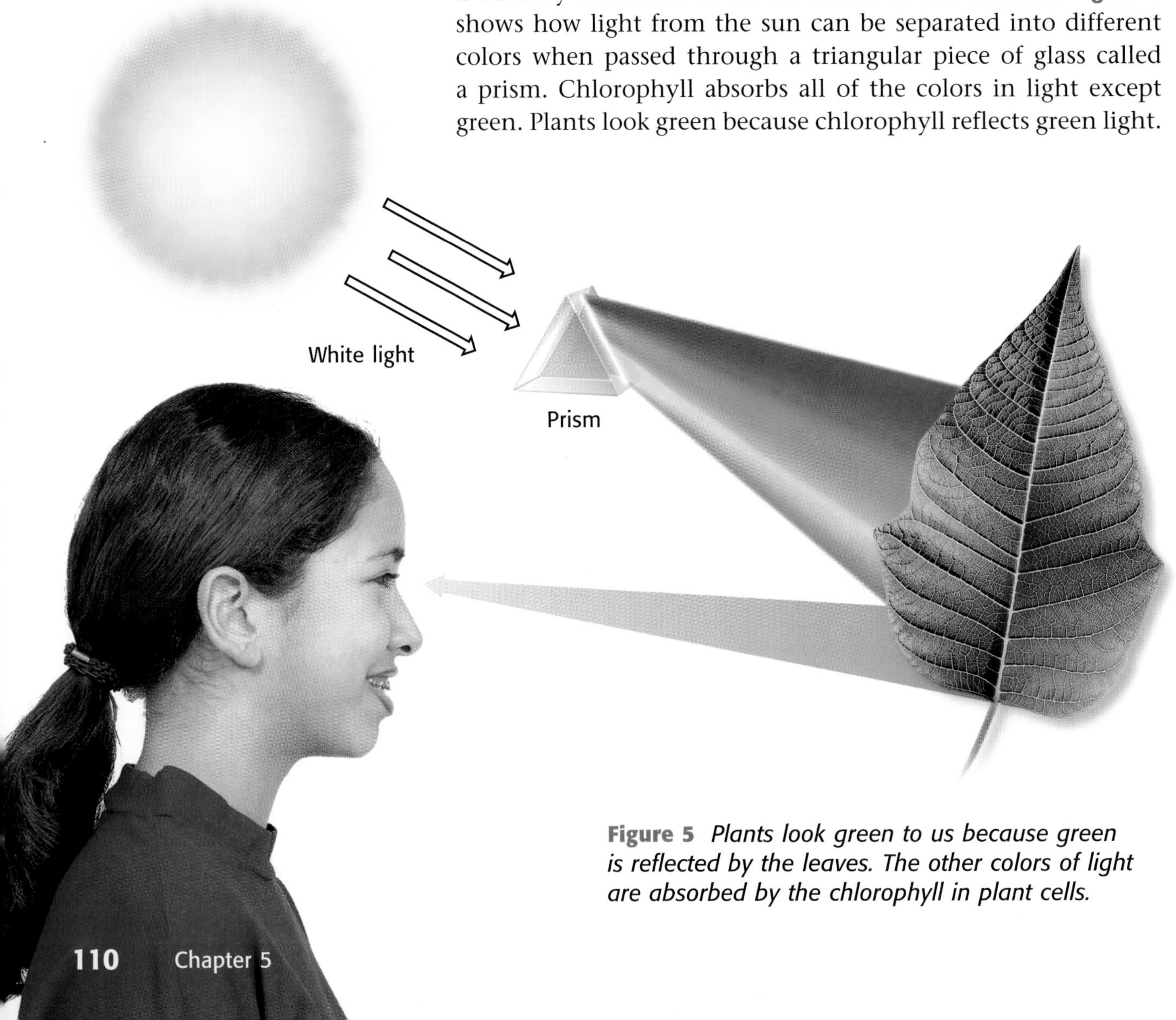

White light

Prism

Figure 5 *Plants look green to us because green is reflected by the leaves. The other colors of light are absorbed by the chlorophyll in plant cells.*

Making Sugar The light energy absorbed by chlorophyll is used to break water (H_2O) down into hydrogen (H) and oxygen (O). The hydrogen is then combined with carbon dioxide (CO_2) from the air to make a sugar called glucose ($C_6H_{12}O_6$). Oxygen is given off as a byproduct. The process of photosynthesis is summarized in the following chemical equation:

$$6CO_2 + 6H_2O \xrightarrow{\text{light energy}} C_6H_{12}O_6 + 6O_2$$

The equation shows that it takes six molecules of carbon dioxide and six molecules of water to produce one molecule of glucose and six molecules of oxygen. The process is illustrated in **Figure 6.**

The energy stored in food molecules is used by plant cells to carry out their life processes. Within each living cell, glucose and other food molecules are broken down in a process called cellular respiration. **Cellular respiration** converts the energy stored in food into a form of energy that cells can use. During this process, the plant uses oxygen and releases carbon dioxide and water.

Self-Check

What is the original source of the energy stored in the sugar produced by plant cells? *(See page 168 to check your answer.)*

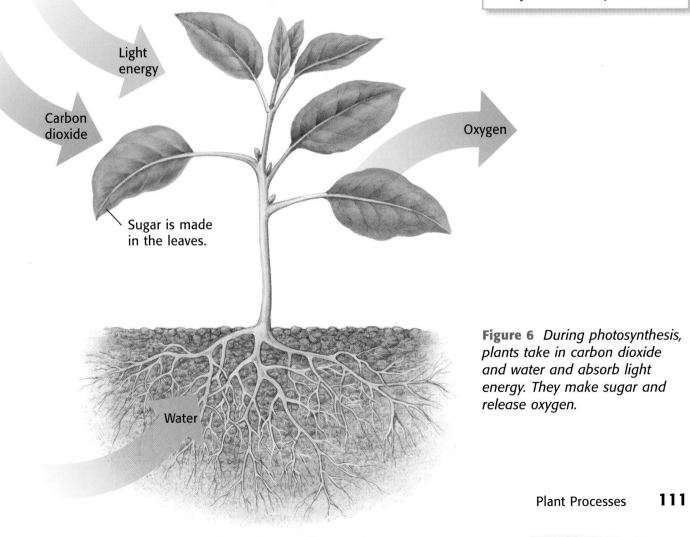

Light energy

Carbon dioxide

Oxygen

Sugar is made in the leaves.

Water

Figure 6 During photosynthesis, plants take in carbon dioxide and water and absorb light energy. They make sugar and release oxygen.

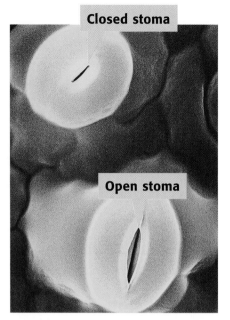

Closed stoma

Open stoma

Figure 7 *When light is available for photosynthesis, the stomata are usually open. When it's dark, the stomata close to conserve water.*

Gas Exchange

All above ground plant surfaces are covered by a waxy cuticle. How does a plant obtain carbon dioxide through this barrier? Carbon dioxide enters the plant's leaves through the **stomata** (singular, *stoma*). A stoma is an opening in the leaf's epidermis and cuticle. Each stoma is surrounded by two *guard cells,* which act like double doors, opening and closing the gap. You can see open and closed stomata in **Figure 7.** The function of stomata is shown in **Figure 8.**

When the stomata are open, carbon dioxide diffuses into the leaf. The oxygen produced during photosynthesis diffuses out of the leaf cells and exits the leaf through the stomata.

When the stomata are open, water vapor also exits the leaf. The loss of water from leaves is called **transpiration.** Most of the water absorbed by a plant's roots is needed to replace water lost during transpiration. When a plant wilts, it is usually because more water is being lost through its leaves than is being absorbed by its roots.

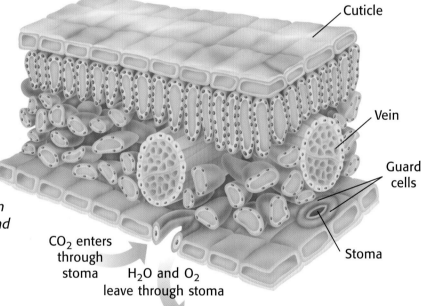

Cuticle

Vein

Guard cells

Stoma

CO₂ enters through stoma

H₂O and O₂ leave through stoma

Figure 8 *Plants take in carbon dioxide and release oxygen and water through the stomata in their leaves.*

SECTION REVIEW

1. What three things do plants need to carry out photosynthesis?

2. Why must plant cells carry out cellular respiration?

3. **Identifying Relationships** How are the opening and closing of stomata related to transpiration? When does transpiration occur?

What You'll Do

◆ Describe how plants may respond to light and gravity.
◆ Explain how some plants flower in response to night length.
◆ Describe how some plants are adapted to survive cold weather.

MATH BREAK

Bending by Degrees

Suppose a plant has a positive phototropism and bends toward the light at a rate of 0.3 degrees per minute. How many hours will it take the plant to bend 90 degrees?

Plant Responses to the Environment

What happens when you get really cold? Do your teeth chatter as you shiver uncontrollably? If so, your brain is responding to the stimulus of cold by causing your muscles to twitch rapidly and generate warmth. Anything that causes a reaction in an organ or tissue is a stimulus. Do plant tissues respond to stimuli? They sure do! Examples of stimuli to which plants respond include light, gravity, and changing seasons.

Plant Tropisms

Some plants respond to an environmental stimulus, such as light or gravity, by growing in a particular direction. Growth in response to a stimulus is called a **tropism.** Tropisms are either positive or negative, depending on whether the plant grows toward or away from the stimulus. Plant growth toward a stimulus is a positive tropism. Plant growth away from a stimulus is a negative tropism. Two examples of tropisms are phototropism and gravitropism.

Sensing Light If you place a houseplant so that it gets light from only one direction, such as from a window, the shoot tips bend toward the light. A change in the growth of a plant that is caused by light is called **phototropism** (foh TAH troh PIZ uhm). As shown in **Figure 9,** the bending occurs when cells on one side of the shoot grow longer than cells on the other side of the shoot.

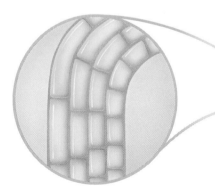

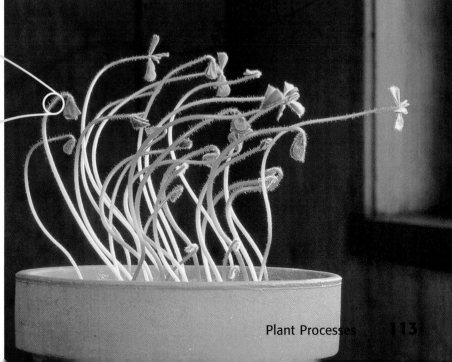

Figure 9 *The plant cells on the dark side of the shoot grow longer than the cells on the other side. This causes the shoot to bend toward the light.*

Plant Processes   **113**

Which Way Is Up? When the growth of a plant changes direction in response to the direction of gravity, the change is called **gravitropism** (GRAV i TROH PIZ uhm). The effect of gravitropism is demonstrated by the plants in **Figure 10.** A few days after a plant is placed on its side or turned upside down, the roots and shoots show a change in their direction of growth. Most shoot tips have negative gravitropism—they grow upward, away from the center of the Earth. In contrast, most root tips have positive gravitropism—they grow downward, toward the center of the Earth.

Figure 10 *Gravity is a stimulus that causes plants to change their direction of growth.*

▲ To grow away from the pull of gravity, this plant has grown upward.

This plant has recently ▶ been upside down.

Which Way Is Up?

Will a potted plant grow sideways? You will need **several potted plants** to find out. Use **duct tape** to secure **cardboard** around the base of each plant so that the soil will not fall out. Turn the plants on their sides and observe what happens over the next few days. Describe two stimuli that might have influenced the direction of growth. How might gravitropism benefit a plant?

✓ Self-Check

1. Use the following terms to create a concept map: tropism, stimuli, light, gravity, phototropism, and gravitropism.

2. Imagine a plant in which light causes a negative phototropism. Will the plant bend to the left or to the right when light is shining only on the plant's right side?

(See page 168 to check your answers.)

Seasonal Responses

What would happen if a plant living in an area that has severe winters flowered in December? Would the plant be able to successfully produce seeds and fruits? If your answer is no, you're correct. If the plant produced any flowers at all, the flowers would probably freeze and die before they had the chance to produce mature seeds. Plants living in regions with cold winters can detect the change in seasons. How do plants do this?

As Different as Night and Day Think about what happens as the seasons change. For example, what happens to the length of the days and the nights? As autumn and winter approach, the days get shorter and the nights get longer. The opposite happens when spring and summer approach.

The difference between day length and night length is an important environmental stimulus for many plants. This stimulus can cause plants to begin reproducing. Some plants flower only in late summer or early autumn, when the night length is long. These plants are called short-day plants. Examples of short-day plants include poinsettias (shown in **Figure 11**), ragweed, and chrysanthemums. Other plants flower in spring or early summer, when night length is short. These plants are called long-day plants. Clover, spinach, and lettuce are examples of long-day plants.

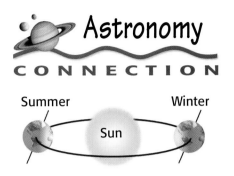

Astronomy

CONNECTION

Summer · · · · · · · · · · · Winter

Sun

The seasons are caused by Earth's tilt and its orbit around the sun. We have summer when the Northern Hemisphere is tilted toward the sun and the sun's energy falls more directly on the Northern Hemisphere. While the Northern Hemisphere experiences the warm season, the Southern Hemisphere experiences the cold season. The opposite of this occurs when the Northern Hemisphere is tilted away from the sun.

Figure 11 *Night length determines when poinsettias flower.*

Early summer

Night length

Day length

◄ In the early summer, night length is short. At this time, poinsettia leaves are all green, and there are no flowers.

Late fall

Night length

Day length

◄ Poinsettias flower in the fall, when nights are longer. The leaves surrounding the flower clusters turn red. Professional growers use artificial lighting to control the timing of the color change.

Can Trees Tell Time?

One fall afternoon, Holly looks into her backyard. She notices that a tree that was full of leaves the week before is now completely bare. What caused the tree to drop all its leaves?

Holly came up with the following hypothesis:

Each leaf on the tree was able to sense day length. When the day length became short enough, each leaf responded by falling.

Design an experiment that would test Holly's hypothesis.

Seasonal Changes in Leaves All trees lose their leaves at some time. Some trees, such as pine and holly, shed some of their leaves year-round so that some leaves are always present on the tree. These trees are called **evergreen.** Evergreen trees have leaves adapted to survive throughout the year.

Other trees, such as the maple tree in **Figure 12,** are **deciduous** and lose all their leaves at the same time each year. Deciduous trees usually lose their leaves before winter begins. In tropical climates that have wet and dry seasons, deciduous trees lose their leaves before the dry season. Having bare branches during the winter or during the dry season may reduce the water lost by transpiration. The loss of leaves helps plants survive low temperatures or long periods without rain.

Figure 12 *The leaves of some deciduous trees, like the maple shown here, change from green to orange in autumn. In winter, the maple is bare.*

As shown in **Figure 13,** leaves often change color before they fall. As autumn approaches, chlorophyll, the green pigment used in photosynthesis, breaks down. As chlorophyll is lost from leaves, other yellow and orange pigments are revealed. These pigments were always present in the leaves but were hidden by the green chlorophyll. Some leaves also have red pigments, which also become visible when chlorophyll is broken down.

BRAIN FOOD

In autumn, trees growing near streetlights keep their leaves longer than their rural counterparts.

Figure 13 *The breakdown of chlorophyll in the autumn is a seasonal response in many trees. As the amount of chlorophyll in leaves decreases, other pigments become visible.*

SECTION REVIEW

1. What are the effects of the tropisms caused by light and gravity?

2. What is the difference between a short-day plant and a long-day plant?

3. How does the loss of leaves help a plant survive winter or long periods without rain?

4. **Applying Concepts** If a plant does not flower when exposed to 12 hours of daylight but does flower when exposed to 15 hours of daylight, is it a short-day plant or a long-day plant?

Food Factory Waste

Plants use photosynthesis to produce food. We cannot live without the waste products from this process. In this activity, you will observe the process of photosynthesis and determine the rate of photosynthesis for *Elodea.*

MATERIALS

- 500 mL of 5% baking soda-and-water solution
- 600 mL beaker
- 20 cm long *Elodea* sprigs (2–3)
- glass funnel
- test tube
- metric ruler

Procedure

1. Add 450 mL of baking soda–and–water solution to a beaker.

2. Put two or three sprigs of *Elodea* in the beaker. The baking soda will provide the *Elodea* with the carbon dioxide it needs for photosynthesis.

3. Place the wide end of the funnel over the *Elodea.* The end of the funnel with the small opening should be pointing up. The *Elodea* and the funnel should be completely covered by the solution.

4. Fill a test tube with the remaining baking soda–and–water solution. Place your thumb over the end of the test tube. Turn the test tube upside down, taking care that no air enters. Hold the opening of the test tube under the solution and place the test tube over the small end of the funnel. Try not to let any solution out of the test tube as you do this.

5. Place the beaker setup in a well-lit area near a lamp or in direct sunlight.

6. Prepare a data table similar to the one below.

Amount of Gas Present in the Test Tube		
Days of exposure to light	Total amount of gas present (mm)	Amount of gas produced per day (mm)
0		
1		
2		
3		
4		
5		

DO NOT WRITE IN BOOK

7 Record that there was 0 mm of gas in the test tube on day 0. (If you were unable to place the test tube without getting air in the tube, measure the height of the column of air in the test tube in millimeters. Record this value for day 0.) Measure the gas in the test tube from the middle of the curve on the bottom of the upside-down test tube to the level of the solution.

8 For days 1 through 5, measure the amount of gas in the test tube. Record the measurements in your data table under the heading "Total amount of gas present (mm)."

9 Calculate the amount of gas produced each day by subtracting the amount of gas present on the previous day from the amount of gas present today. Record these amounts under the heading "Amount of gas produced per day (mm)."

10 Plot the data from your table on a graph.

Analysis

11 Using information from your graph, describe what happened to the amount of gas in the test tube.

12 How much gas was produced in the test tube after day 5?

13 Write the equation for photosynthesis. Explain each part of the equation. For example, what "ingredients" are necessary for photosynthesis to take place? What substances are produced by photosynthesis? What gas is produced that we need in order to live?

14 Write a report describing your experiment, your results, and your conclusions.

Going Further
Hydroponics is the growing of plants in nutrient-rich water. Research hydroponic techniques, and try to grow a plant without soil.

Chapter Highlights

SECTION 1

Vocabulary

dormant *(p. 108)*

Section Notes

- Sexual reproduction in flowering plants requires pollination and fertilization. Fertilization is the joining of an egg and a sperm cell.

- After fertilization has occurred, the ovules develop into seeds that contain plant embryos. The ovary develops into a fruit.

- Once seeds mature, they may become dormant. Seeds sprout when they are in an environment with the proper temperature and the proper amounts of water and oxygen.

- Many flowering plants can reproduce asexually without flowers.

SECTION 2

Vocabulary

chlorophyll *(p. 110)*

cellular respiration *(p. 111)*

stomata *(p. 112)*

transpiration *(p. 112)*

Section Notes

- During photosynthesis, leaves absorb sunlight and form glucose from carbon dioxide and water.

- During cellular respiration, a plant uses oxygen and releases carbon dioxide and water. Glucose is converted into a form of energy that cells can use.

- Plants take in carbon dioxide and release oxygen and water through stomata in their leaves.

Labs

Weepy Weeds *(p. 138)*

☑ Skills Check

Visual Understanding

CIRCLE GRAPH A circle graph is a great visual for illustrating fractions without using numbers. Each circle graph on page 115 represents a 24-hour period. The blue area represents the fraction of time in which there is no sunlight, and the gold area represents the fraction of time in which there is light. As shown by the graph, early summer is about two-thirds day and one-third night.

BAR GRAPHS As shown on page 117, bar graphs are often used to compare numbers. The graph at right compares the success rate of flower seeds from five seed producers. As shown by the bar height, company D, at about 88 percent, had the highest rate of success.

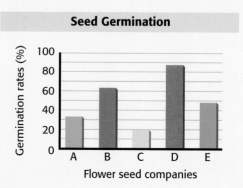

Seed Germination

Germination rates (%)

Flower seed companies

Vocabulary

tropism *(p. 113)*
phototropism *(p. 113)*
gravitropism *(p. 114)*
evergreen *(p. 116)*
deciduous *(p. 116)*

Section Notes

- A tropism is plant growth in response to an environmental stimulus, such as light or gravity. Plant growth toward a stimulus is a positive tropism. Plant growth away from a stimulus is a negative tropism.

- Phototropism is growth in response to the direction of light. Gravitropism is growth in response to the direction of gravity.

- The change in the amount of daylight and darkness that occurs with changing seasons often controls plant reproduction.

- Evergreen plants have leaves adapted to survive throughout the year. Deciduous plants lose their leaves before cold or dry seasons. The loss of leaves helps deciduous plants survive low temperatures and dry periods.

---

internet**connect**

GO TO: go.hrw.com

*SCI*LINKS.*

N S T A

GO TO: www.scilinks.org

Visit the **HRW** Web site for a variety of learning tools related to this chapter. Just type in the keyword:

KEYWORD: HSTPL2

Visit the **National Science Teachers Association** on-line Web site for Internet resources related to this chapter. Just type in the *sci*LINKS number for more information about the topic:

TOPIC: Reproduction of Plants	***sci*LINKS NUMBER:** HSTL305
TOPIC: Photosynthesis	***sci*LINKS NUMBER:** HSTL310
TOPIC: Plant Tropisms	***sci*LINKS NUMBER:** HSTL315
TOPIC: Plant Growth	***sci*LINKS NUMBER:** HSTL320

Chapter Review

USING VOCABULARY

To complete the following sentences, choose the correct term from each pair of terms listed below:

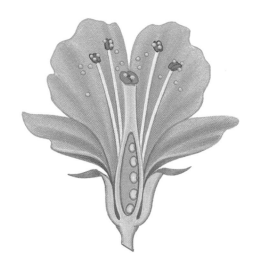

1. After seeds develop fully, and before they sprout, they may become ___?___. *(deciduous* or *dormant)*

2. During ___?___, energy from sunlight is used to make sugar. *(photosynthesis* or *phototropism)*

3. The loss of water through stomata is called ___?___. *(transpiration* or *tropism)*

4. A change in plant growth in response to the direction of light is called ___?___. *(gravitropism* or *phototropism)*

5. Plants that have leaves year-round are ___?___. *(deciduous* or *evergreen)*

UNDERSTANDING CONCEPTS

Multiple Choice

6. The cells that open and close the stomata are the
   a. guard cells.
   b. xylem cells.
   c. cuticle cells.
   d. mesophyll cells.

7. Plant cells need carbon dioxide, which is used for
   a. cellular respiration. c. fertilization.
   b. phototropism. d. photosynthesis.

8. When chlorophyll breaks down,
   a. pollination occurs.
   b. other pigments become visible.
   c. red pigments disappear.
   d. photosynthesis occurs.

9. Which of the following sequences shows the correct order of events that occur after an insect brings pollen to a flower?
   a. germination, fertilization, pollination
   b. fertilization, germination, pollination
   c. pollination, germination, fertilization
   d. pollination, fertilization, germination

10. When the amount of water transpired from a plant's leaves is greater than the amount absorbed by its roots,
    a. the cuticle conserves water.
    b. the stem exhibits positive gravitropism.
    c. the plant wilts.
    d. the plant recovers from wilting.

11. Ovules develop into
    a. fruits.   c. flowers.
    b. ovaries.   d. seeds.

Short Answer

12. What is the relationship between transpiration, the cuticle, and the stomata?

13. What is the stimulus in phototropism? What is the plant's response to the stimulus?

14. Give an example of a positive tropism and a negative tropism.

Concept Mapping

15. Use the following terms to create a concept map: plantlets, flower, seeds, ovules, plant reproduction, asexual, runners.

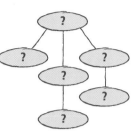

CRITICAL THINKING AND PROBLEM SOLVING

Write one or two sentences to answer the following questions:

16. Many plants that live in regions that experience severe winters have seeds that will not germinate at any temperature unless the seeds have been exposed first to a long period of cold. How might this characteristic help new plants survive?

17. If you wanted to make poinsettias bloom and turn red in the summer, what would you have to do?

18. What benefit is there for a plant's shoots to have positive phototropism? What benefit is there for its roots to have positive gravitropism?

MATH IN SCIENCE

19. If a particular leaf has a surface area of 8 cm², what is its surface area in square millimeters? (Hint: 1 cm² = 100 mm².)

20. Leaves have an average of 100 stomata per square millimeter of surface area. How many stomata would you expect the leaf in question 19 to possess?

INTERPRETING GRAPHICS

The plant hormone involved in phototropism is produced in the shoot tip. The illustration below shows part of an experiment on phototropism. In part (1), the young plants have recently been placed in the light. The shoot tip of one plant is cut off. The other tip is not cut. In part (2), the plants are exposed to light from one direction. Use the picture to answer the questions that follow.

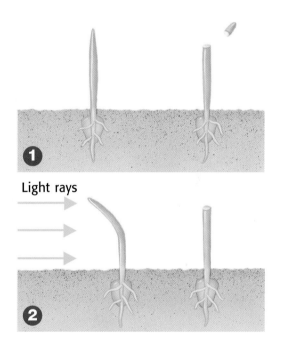

21. Why did the plant with the intact tip bend toward the light?

22. Why did the plant with the removed tip remain straight?

Reading Check-up

Take a minute to review your answers to the Pre-Reading Questions found at the bottom of page 104. Have your answers changed? If necessary, revise your answers based on what you have learned since you began this chapter.

MUTANT MUSTARD

The tiny mustard flowers grown by Elliot Meyerowitz are horribly deformed. You may think they are the result of a terrible accident, but Meyerowitz created these mutants on purpose. In fact, he is very proud of these flowers because they may help him solve an important biological mystery.

▲ *Elliot Meyerowitz, shown here in his laboratory, has raised about a million individual specimens of a mustard variety known as Arabidopsis thaliana.*

Normal and Abnormal Flowers

Normally, mustard flowers have four distinct parts that are arranged in a specific way. Many of the plants grown by Meyerowitz and his colleagues, however, are far from normal. Some have leaves in the center of their flowers. Others have seed-producing ovaries where the petals should be. At first glance, the arrangement of the parts seems random, but the structure of each flower has actually been determined by a small number of genes.

A Simple Model

After many years of careful studies, Meyerowitz and his colleagues have identified most of the genes that control the mustard flower's development. With this information, Meyerowitz has discovered patterns that have led to a surprisingly simple model. The model

points to just three classes of genes that determine what happens to the various parts of a flower as it develops. He learned that if one or more of those gene classes is inactivated, a mutant mustard plant results.

Pieces of an Old Puzzle

By understanding how genes shape the growth of flowers, Meyerowitz hopes to add pieces to a long-standing puzzle involving the origin of flowering plants. Scientists estimate that flowering plants first appeared on Earth about 125 million years ago and that they quickly spread to become the dominant plants on Earth. By studying which genes produce flowers in present-day plants, Meyerowitz and his colleagues hope to learn how flowering plants evolved in the first place.

Meyerowitz's mutant plants are well qualified to add to our understanding of plant genetics. But don't look for these mustard plants in your local flower shop. These strange mutants won't win any prizes for beauty!

▲ *Meyerowitz alters the genes of a mustard plant so that it develops a mutant flower. The inset shows a normal flower.*

Think About It

▶ It is possible to genetically change a plant. What are some possible risks of such a practice?

EYE ON THE ENVIRONMENT

A Rainbow of Cotton

Think about your favorite T-shirt. Chances are, it's made of cotton and brightly colored. The fibers in cotton plants, however, are naturally white. They must be dyed with chemicals—often toxic ones—to create the bright colors seen in T-shirts and other fabrics. To minimize the use of toxic chemicals, an ingenious woman named Sally Fox had an idea: What if you could grow the cotton *already colored*?

Learning from the Past

Cotton fibers come from the plant's seed pods, or *bolls.* Bolls are a little bigger than a golf ball and open at maturity to reveal a fuzzy mass of fibers and seeds. Once the seeds are removed, the fibers can be twisted into yarn and used to make many kinds of fabric. Sally Fox began her career as an *entomologist,* a scientist who studies insects. She first found out about colored cotton while studying pest resistance. Although most of the cotton grown for textiles is white, different shades of cotton have been harvested by Native Americans for centuries. These types of cotton showed some resistance to pests but had fibers too short to be used by the textile industry.

In 1982, Fox began the very slow process of crossbreeding different varieties of cotton to produce strains that were both colored *and* long-fibered. Her cotton is registered under the name FoxFibre® and has earned her high praise.

Solutions to Environmental Problems

The textile industry is the source of two major environmental hazards. The first hazard is the dyes used for cotton fabrics. The second is the pesticides that are required for growing cotton. These pesticides, like the dyes, can cause damage to both living things and natural resources, such as water and land.

Fox's cotton represents a solution to both of these problems. First, since the cotton is naturally colored, no dyes are necessary. Second, the native strains of cotton from which she bred her plants passed on their natural pest resistance. Thus, fewer pesticides are necessary to grow her cotton successfully.

Sally Fox's efforts demonstrate that with ingenuity and patience, science and agriculture can work together in new ways to offer solutions to environmental problems.

▲ *Sally Fox in a field of colored cotton*

Some Detective Work

▶ Like Fox's cotton, many types of plants and breeds of domesticated animals have been created through artificial selection. Research to find out where and when your favorite fruit or breed of dog was first established.

Exploring, inventing, and investigating are essential to the study of science. However, these activities can also be dangerous. To make sure that your experiments and explorations are safe, you must be aware of a variety of safety guidelines.

You have probably heard of the saying, "It is better to be safe than sorry." This is particularly true in a science classroom where experiments and explorations are being performed. Being uninformed and careless can result in serious injuries. Don't take chances with your own safety or with anyone else's.

Following are important guidelines for staying safe in the science classroom. Your teacher may also have safety guidelines and tips that are specific to your classroom and laboratory. Take the time to be safe.

Safety Rules!

Start Out Right

Always get your teacher's permission before attempting any laboratory exploration. Read the procedures carefully, and pay particular attention to safety information and caution statements. If you are unsure about what a safety symbol means, look it up or ask your teacher. You cannot be too careful when it comes to safety. If an accident does occur, inform your teacher immediately, regardless of how minor you think the accident is.

Safety Symbols

All of the experiments and investigations in this book and their related worksheets include important safety symbols to alert you to particular safety concerns. Become familiar with these symbols so that when you see them, you will know what they mean and what to do. It is important that you read this entire safety section to learn about specific dangers in the laboratory.

If you are instructed to note the odor of a substance, wave the fumes toward your nose with your hand. Never put your nose close to the source.

Eye protection

Clothing protection

Hand safety

Heating safety

Electric safety

Chemical safety

Animal safety

Sharp object

Plant safety

Eye Safety

Wear safety goggles when working around chemicals, acids, bases, or any type of flame or heating device. Wear safety goggles any time there is even the slightest chance that harm could come to your eyes. If any substance gets into your eyes, notify your teacher immediately, and flush your eyes with running water for at least 15 minutes. Treat any unknown chemical as if it were a dangerous chemical. Never look directly into the sun. Doing so could cause permanent blindness.

Avoid wearing contact lenses in a laboratory situation. Even if you are wearing safety goggles, chemicals can get between the contact lenses and your eyes. If your doctor requires that you wear contact lenses instead of glasses, wear eye-cup safety goggles in the lab.

Safety Equipment

Know the locations of the nearest fire alarms and any other safety equipment, such as fire blankets and eyewash fountains, as identified by your teacher, and know the procedures for using them.

Be extra careful when using any glassware. When adding a heavy object to a graduated cylinder, tilt the cylinder so the object slides slowly to the bottom.

Neatness

Keep your work area free of all unnecessary books and papers. Tie back long hair, and secure loose sleeves or other loose articles of clothing, such as ties and bows. Remove dangling jewelry. Don't wear open-toed shoes or sandals in the laboratory. Never eat, drink, or apply cosmetics in a laboratory setting. Food, drink, and cosmetics can easily become contaminated with dangerous materials.

Certain hair products (such as aerosol hair spray) are flammable and should not be worn while working near an open flame. Avoid wearing hair spray or hair gel on lab days.

Sharp/Pointed Objects

Use knives and other sharp instruments with extreme care. Never cut objects while holding them in your hands. Place objects on a suitable work surface for cutting.

Heat

Wear safety goggles when using a heating device or a flame. Whenever possible, use an electric hot plate as a heat source instead of an open flame. When heating materials in a test tube, always angle the test tube away from yourself and others. In order to avoid burns, wear heat-resistant gloves whenever instructed to do so.

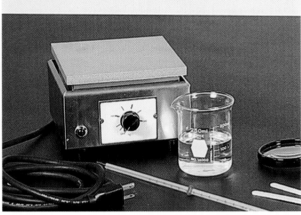

Electricity

Be careful with electrical cords. When using a microscope with a lamp, do not place the cord where it could trip someone. Do not let cords hang over a table edge in a way that could cause equipment to fall if the cord is accidentally pulled. Do not use equipment with damaged cords. Be sure your hands are dry and that the electrical equipment is in the "off" position before plugging it in. Turn off and unplug electrical equipment when you are finished.

Chemicals

Wear safety goggles when handling any potentially dangerous chemicals, acids, or bases. If a chemical is unknown, handle it as you would a dangerous chemical. Wear an apron and safety gloves when working with acids or bases or whenever you are told to do so. If a spill gets on your skin or clothing, rinse it off immediately with water for at least 5 minutes while calling to your teacher.

Never mix chemicals unless your teacher tells you to do so. Never taste, touch, or smell chemicals unless you are specifically directed to do so. Before working with a flammable liquid or gas, check for the presence of any source of flame, spark, or heat.

Animal Safety

Always obtain your teacher's permission before bringing any animal into the school building. Handle animals only as your teacher directs. Always treat animals carefully and with respect. Wash your hands thoroughly after handling any animal.

Plant Safety

Do not eat any part of a plant or plant seed used in the laboratory. Wash hands thoroughly after handling any part of a plant. When in nature, do not pick any wild plants unless your teacher instructs you to do so.

Glassware

Examine all glassware before use. Be sure that glassware is clean and free of chips and cracks. Report damaged glassware to your teacher. Glass containers used for heating should be made of heat-resistant glass.

Does It All Add Up?

Your math teacher won't tell you this, but did you know that sometimes 2 + 2 does not equal 4?! (Well, it really does, but sometimes it doesn't *appear* to equal 4.) In this experiment, you will use the scientific method to predict, measure, and observe the mixing of two unknown liquids. You will learn that a scientist does not set out to prove a hypothesis, but rather to test it, and sometimes the results just don't seem to add up!

Materials

- 75 mL of liquid A
- 75 mL of liquid B
- 100 mL graduated cylinders (7)
- glass-labeling marker
- Celsius thermometer
- protective gloves

Make Observations

1. Examine the two mystery liquids in the graduated cylinders given to you by your teacher.
   Caution: Do not taste, touch, or smell the liquids.

2. In your ScienceLog, write down as many observations as you can about each liquid. Are the liquids bubbly? What color are they? What is the exact volume of each liquid? Touch the graduated cylinders. Are they hot or cold?

3. Pour exactly 25 mL of liquid A into each of two graduated cylinders. Combine these samples in one of the graduated cylinders, and record the final volume in your ScienceLog. Repeat this step for liquid B.

Form a Hypothesis

4. Based on your observations and on prior experience, what do you expect the volume to be when you pour these two liquids together?

Make a Prediction

5. Make a prediction based on your hypothesis using an "if-then" format. Explain why you have made your prediction.

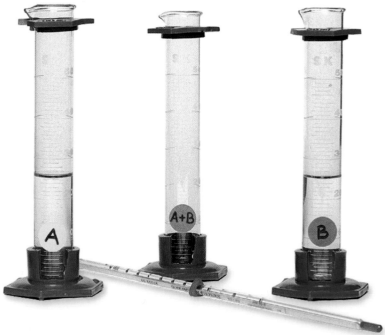

Test the Hypothesis

6. In your ScienceLog, make a data table similar to the one below to record your predictions and observations.

	Contents of cylinder A	Contents of cylinder B	Mixing results: predictions	Mixing results: observations
Volume				
Appearance				
Temperature				

DO NOT WRITE IN BOOK

7. Carefully pour exactly 25 mL of Liquid A into a 50 mL graduated cylinder. Mark this cylinder "A." Record its volume, appearance, and temperature in the data table.

8. Carefully pour exactly 25 mL of Liquid B into another 50 mL graduated cylinder. Mark this cylinder "B." Record its volume, appearance, and temperature in the data table.

9. Mark the empty third cylinder "A + B."

10. In the "Mixing results: predictions" column in your table, record the prediction you made earlier. Each classmate may have made a different prediction.

11. Carefully pour the contents of both cylinders into the third graduated cylinder.

12. Observe and record the total volume, appearance, and temperature in the "Mixing results: observations" column of the table.

Analyze the Results

13. Discuss your predictions as a class. How many different predictions were there? Which predictions were supported by testing? Did any of your measurements surprise you?

Draw Conclusions

14. Was your hypothesis supported? Explain why this may have happened.

15. Explain the value of incorrect predictions.

Graphing Data

When performing an experiment it is usually necessary to collect data. To understand the data, it is often good to organize them into a graph. Graphs can show trends and patterns that you might not notice in a table or list. In this exercise, you will practice collecting data and organizing the data into a graph.

Materials

- 200 mL of water
- 400 mL beaker
- ice
- Celsius thermometer with a clip
- hot plate
- clock or watch with a second hand
- graph paper
- heat-resistant gloves

Procedure

1. Pour 200 mL of water into a 400 mL beaker. Add ice to the beaker until the water line is at the 400 mL mark.

2. Place a Celsius thermometer into the beaker. Use a thermometer clip to prevent the thermometer from touching the bottom of the beaker. Record the temperature of the ice water in your ScienceLog.

3. Place the beaker and thermometer on a hot plate. Turn the hot plate on medium heat and record the temperature every minute until the water temperature reaches 100°C.

4. Using heat-resistant gloves, remove the beaker from the hot plate. Continue to record the temperature of the water each minute for 10 more minutes.
   Caution: Don't forget to turn off the hot plate.

5. On a piece of graph paper, create a graph similar to the one below. Label the horizontal axis (the *x*-axis) "Time (min)," and mark the axis in increments of 1 minute as shown. Label the vertical axis (the *y*-axis) "Temperature (°C)," and mark the axis in increments of ten degrees as shown.

6. Find the 1-minute mark on the *x*-axis, and move up the graph to the temperature you recorded at 1 minute. Place a dot on the graph at that point. Plot each temperature in the same way. When you have plotted all of your data, connect the dots with a smooth line.

Analysis

7. Examine your graph. Do you think the water heated faster than it cooled? Explain.

8. Estimate what the temperature of the water was 2.5 minutes after you placed the beaker on the hot plate. Explain how you can make a good estimate of temperature between those you recorded.

9. Explain how a graph may give more information than the same data in a chart.

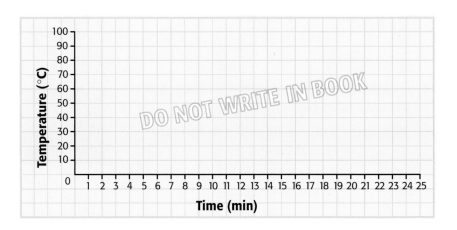

A Window to a Hidden World

Have you ever noticed that objects underwater appear closer than they really are? That's because light waves change speed when they travel from air into water. Anton van Leeuwenhoek, a pioneer of microscopy in the late seventeenth century, used a drop of water to magnify objects. That drop of water brought a hidden world closer into view. How did Leeuwenhoek's microscope work? In this investigation, you will build a model of it to find out.

Materials

- hole punch
- 3 × 10 cm piece of poster board
- clear plastic wrap
- transparent tape
- eyedropper
- water
- newspaper

Procedure

1. Punch a hole in the center of the poster board with a hole punch, as shown in (a) at right.

2. Tape a small piece of clear plastic wrap over the hole, as shown in (b) at right. Be sure the plastic wrap is large enough so that the tape you use to secure it does not cover the hole.

3. Use an eyedropper to put one drop of water over the hole. Check to be sure your drop of water is dome-shaped (convex), as shown in (c) at right.

4. Hold the microscope close to your eye and look through the drop. Be careful not to disturb the water drop.

5. Hold the microscope over a piece of newspaper and observe the image.

Analysis

6. Describe and draw the image you see. Is the image larger or the same size as it was without the microscope? Is the image clear or blurred? Is the shape of the image distorted?

7. How do you think your model could be improved?

Going Further

Robert Hooke and Zacharias Janssen contributed much to the field of microscopy. Find out who they were, when they lived, and what they did.

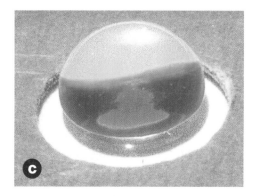

The Best-Bread Bakery Dilemma

The chief baker at the Best-Bread Bakery thinks that the yeast the bakery received may be dead. Yeast is a central ingredient in bread. Yeast is a living organism, a member of the kingdom Fungi, and it undergoes the same life processes as other living organisms. When yeast grows in the presence of oxygen and other nutrients, it produces carbon dioxide. The gas forms bubbles that cause the dough to rise. Thousands of dollars may be lost if the yeast is dead.

The Best-Bread Bakery has requested that you test the yeast. The bakery has furnished samples of live yeast and some samples of the yeast in question.

Materials

- yeast samples (live, A, and B)
- magnifying lens
- test tubes or clear plastic cups
- test-tube rack
- 250 mL beaker
- 125 mL of water
- hot plate
- Celsius thermometer with clip
- scoopula or small spoon
- sugar
- graduated cylinder
- 3 wooden stirring sticks
- flour
- heat-resistant gloves

Procedure

1. Make a data table similar to the one below. Leave plenty of room to write your observations.

2. Examine each yeast sample with a magnifying lens. You may want to sniff the samples to determine the presence of an odor. (Your teacher will demonstrate the appropriate way to detect odors in the laboratory.) Record your observations in the data table.

3. Label three test tubes or plastic cups "Live Yeast," "Sample A Yeast," and "Sample B Yeast."

4. Fill a beaker with 125 mL of water, and place the beaker on a hot plate. Use a thermometer to be sure the water does not get warmer than 32°C. Attach the thermometer to the side of the beaker with a clip so the thermometer doesn't touch the bottom of the beaker. Turn off the hot plate when the temperature reaches 32°C.

	Observations	0 min	5 min	10 min	15 min	20 min	25 min	Dead or alive?
Live yeast								
Sample A yeast								
Sample B yeast								

DO NOT WRITE IN BOOK

5. Add a small scoop (about $\frac{1}{2}$ tsp) of each yeast sample to the correctly labeled container. Add a small scoop of sugar to each container.

6. Add 10 mL of the warm water to each container, and stir.

7. Add a small scoop of flour to each container, and stir again. The flour will help make the process more visible but is not necessary as food for the yeast.

8. Observe the samples carefully. Look for bubbles. Make observations at 5-minute intervals. Write your observations in the data table.

9. In the last column of the data table, write "alive" or "dead" based on your observations during the experiment.

Analysis

10. Describe any differences in the yeast samples before the experiment.

11. Describe the appearance of the yeast samples at the conclusion of the experiment.

12. Why was a sample of live yeast included in the experiment?

13. Why was sugar added to the samples?

14. Based on your observations, is either sample alive?

15. Write a letter to the Best-Bread Bakery stating your recommendation to use or not use the yeast samples. Give reasons for your recommendation.

Going Further

Based on your observations of the nutrient requirements of yeast, design an experiment to determine the ideal combination of nutrients. Vary the amount of nutrients or examine different energy sources.

Aunt Flossie and the Intruder

DESIGN YOUR OWN

Aunt Flossie is a *really* bad housekeeper! She *never* cleans the refrigerator, and things get really gross in there. Last week she pulled out a plastic resealable bag that looked like it was going to explode! The bag was full of gas that she did not put there! Aunt Flossie remembered from her school days that gases are released from living things as waste products. Something had to be alive in the bag! Aunt Flossie became very upset that there was an intruder in her refrigerator. She said she would not bake another cookie until you determine the nature of the intruder.

Materials

- items to be determined by the students and approved by teacher as needed for each experiment such as resealable plastic bags, food samples, a scale, or a thermometer.

- protective gloves

Procedure

1. Design an investigation to determine how gas got into Aunt Flossie's bag. In your ScienceLog, make a list of the materials you will need, and prepare all the data tables you will need for recording your observations.

2. As you design your investigation, be sure to include each of the steps listed at right.

3. Get your teacher's approval of your experimental design and your list of materials before you begin.

4. Dispose of your materials according to your teacher's instructions at the end of your experiment.
   Caution: Do not open any bags of spoiled food or allow any of the contents to escape.

- Ask a question
- Form a hypothesis
- Test the hypothesis
- Analyze the data
- Draw conclusions
- Communicate your results

Analysis

5. Write a letter to Aunt Flossie describing your experiment. Explain what produced the gas in the bag and your recommendations for preventing these intruders in her refrigerator in the future. Invite her to bake cookies for your class!

Going Further

Research in the library or on the Internet to find out how people kept food fresh before refrigeration. Find out what advances have been made in food preservation as a result of the space program.

Travelin' Seeds

You have learned from your study of plants that there are some very interesting and unusual plant adaptations. Some of the most interesting adaptations are modifications that allow plant seeds and fruits to be dispersed, or scattered, away from the parent plant. This dispersal enables the young seedlings to obtain the space, sun, and other resources they need without directly competing with the parent plant.

In this activity, you will use your own creativity to disperse a seed.

Materials

- bean seed
- seed-dispersal challenge card
- various household or recycled materials (examples: glue, tape, paper, paper clips, rubber bands, cloth, paper cups and plates, paper towels, cardboard)

Procedure

1. Obtain a seed and a dispersal challenge card from your teacher. In your ScienceLog, record the type of challenge card you have been given.

2. Create a plan for using the available materials to disperse your seed as described on the challenge card. Record your plan in your ScienceLog. Get your teacher's approval before proceeding.

3. With your teacher's permission, test your seed-dispersal method. Perform several trials. Make a data table in your ScienceLog, and record the results of your trials.

◄ Mangrove seed

Analysis

4. Were you able to successfully complete the seed-dispersal challenge? Explain.

5. Are there any modifications you could make to your method to improve the dispersal of your seed?

6. Describe some plants that disperse their seeds in a way similar to your seed-dispersal method.

◄ Cottonwood

Wild berry ►

Grass bur ►

Weepy Weeds

You are trying to find a way to drain an area that is flooded with water polluted with fertilizer. You know that a plant releases water through the stomata in its leaves. As water evaporates from the leaves, more water is pulled up from the roots through the stem and into the leaves. By this process, called transpiration, water and nutrients are pulled into the plant from the soil. About 90 percent of the water a plant takes up through its roots is released into the atmosphere as water vapor through transpiration. Your idea is to add plants to the flooded area that will transpire the water and take up the fertilizer in their roots.

How much water can a plant take up and release in a certain period of time? In this activity, you will observe transpiration and determine one stem's rate of transpiration.

Materials

- 2 test tubes
- test-tube rack
- water
- coleus or other plant stem cutting
- glass-marking pen
- metric ruler
- clock
- graph paper

Procedure

1. In your ScienceLog, make a data table similar to the one below for recording your measurements.

Height of Water in Test Tubes		
Time	Test tube with plant	Test tube without plant
Initial		
After 10 min		
After 20 min		
After 30 min		
After 40 min		
Overnight		

DO NOT WRITE IN BOOK

2. Fill each test tube approximately three-fourths full of water. Place both test tubes in a test-tube rack.

3. Place the plant stem so that it stands upright in one of the test tubes. Your test tubes should look like the ones in the photograph at right.

4. Use the glass-marking pen to mark the water level in each of the test tubes. Be sure you have the plant stem in place in its test tube before you mark the water level. Why is this necessary?

5. Measure the height of the water in each test tube. Be sure to hold the test tube level, and measure from the waterline to the bottom of the curve at the bottom of the test tube. Record these measurements on the row labeled "Initial."

6. Wait 10 minutes, and measure the height of the water in each test tube again. Record these measurements in your data table.

7. Repeat step 6 three more times. Record your measurements each time.

8. Wait 24 hours, and measure the height of the water in each test tube. Record these measurements in your data table.

9. Construct a graph similar to the one below. Plot the data from your data table. Draw a line for each test tube. Use a different color for each line, and make a key below your graph.

10. Calculate the rate of transpiration for your plant by using the following operations:

Test tube with plant:
Initial height
− Overnight height
$\overline{}$
Difference in height of water **(A)**

Test tube without plant:
Initial height
− Overnight height
$\overline{}$
Difference in height of water **(B)**

Water height difference due to transpiration:
Difference **A**
− Difference **B**
$\overline{}$
Water lost due to transpiration (in millimeters) in 24 hours

Analysis

11. What was the purpose of the test tube that held only water?

12. What caused the water to go down in the test tube containing the plant stem? Did the same thing happen in the test tube with water only? Explain your answer.

13. What was the calculated rate of transpiration per day?

14. Using your graph, compare the rate of transpiration with the rate of evaporation alone.

15. Prepare a presentation of your experiment for your class. Use your data tables, graphs, and calculations as visual aids.

Going Further

How many leaves did your plant sprigs have? Use this number to estimate what the rate of transpiration might be for a plant with 200 leaves. When you have your answer in millimeters of height in a test tube, pour this amount into a graduated cylinder to measure it in milliliters.

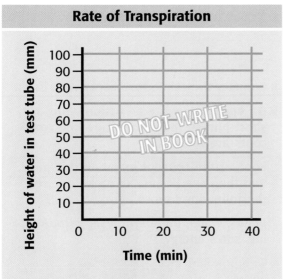

Rate of Transpiration

Height of water in test tube (mm)

100 90 80 70 60 50 40 30 20 10

0   10   20   30   40

Time (min)

DO NOT WRITE IN BOOK

red—test tube without plant
blue—test tube with plant

Concept Mapping: A Way to Bring Ideas Together

What Is a Concept Map?

Have you ever tried to tell someone about a book or a chapter you've just read and found that you can remember only a few isolated words and ideas? Or maybe you've memorized facts for a test and then weeks later discovered you're not even sure what topics those facts covered.

In both cases, you may have understood the ideas or concepts by themselves but not in relation to one another. If you could somehow link the ideas together, you would probably understand them better and remember them longer. This is something a concept map can help you do. A concept map is a way to see how ideas or concepts fit together. It can help you see the "big picture."

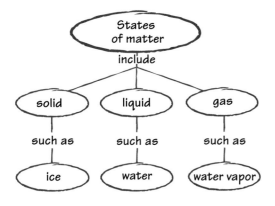

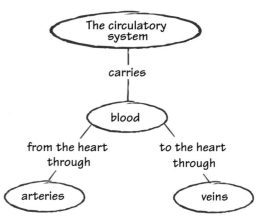

How to Make a Concept Map

❶ Make a list of the main ideas or concepts.

It might help to write each concept on its own slip of paper. This will make it easier to rearrange the concepts as many times as necessary to make sense of how the concepts are connected. After you've made a few concept maps this way, you can go directly from writing your list to actually making the map.

❷ Arrange the concepts in order from the most general to the most specific.

Put the most general concept at the top and circle it. Ask yourself, "How does this concept relate to the remaining concepts?" As you see the relationships, arrange the concepts in order from general to specific.

❸ Connect the related concepts with lines.

❹ On each line, write an action word or short phrase that shows how the concepts are related.

Look at the concept maps on this page, and then see if you can make one for the following terms:

plants, water, photosynthesis, carbon dioxide, sun's energy

One possible answer is provided at right, but don't look at it until you try the concept map yourself.

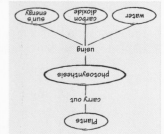

SI Measurement

The International System of Units, or SI, is the standard system of measurement used by many scientists. Using the same standards of measurement makes it easier for scientists to communicate with one another.

SI works by combining prefixes and base units. Each base unit can be used with different prefixes to define smaller and larger quantities. The table below lists common SI prefixes.

SI Prefixes

Prefix	Abbreviation	Factor	Example
kilo-	k	1,000	kilogram, 1 kg = 1,000 g
hecto-	h	100	hectoliter, 1 hL = 100 L
deka-	da	10	dekameter, 1 dam = 10 m
		1	meter, liter
deci-	d	0.1	decigram, 1 dg = 0.1 g
centi-	c	0.01	centimeter, 1 cm = 0.01 m
milli-	m	0.001	milliliter, 1 mL = 0.001 L
micro-	µ	0.000 001	micrometer, 1 µm = 0.000 001 m

SI Conversion Table

SI units	From SI to English	From English to SI
Length		
kilometer (km) = 1,000 m	1 km = 0.621 mi	1 mi = 1.609 km
meter (m) = 100 cm	1 m = 3.281 ft	1 ft = 0.305 m
centimeter (cm) = 0.01 m	1 cm = 0.394 in.	1 in. = 2.540 cm
millimeter (mm) = 0.001 m	1 mm = 0.039 in.	
micrometer (µm) = 0.000 001 m		
nanometer (nm) = 0.000 000 001 m		
Area		
square kilometer (km^2) = 100 hectares	1 km^2 = 0.386 mi^2	1 mi^2 = 2.590 km^2
hectare (ha) = 10,000 m^2	1 ha = 2.471 acres	1 acre = 0.405 ha
square meter (m^2) = 10,000 cm^2	1 m^2 = 10.765 ft^2	1 ft^2 = 0.093 m^2
square centimeter (cm^2) = 100 mm^2	1 cm^2 = 0.155 $in.^2$	1 $in.^2$ = 6.452 cm^2
Volume		
liter (L) = 1,000 mL = 1 dm^3	1 L = 1.057 fl qt	1 fl qt = 0.946 L
milliliter (mL) = 0.001 L = 1 cm^3	1 mL = 0.034 fl oz	1 fl oz = 29.575 mL
microliter (µL) = 0.000 001 L		
Mass		
kilogram (kg) = 1,000 g	1 kg = 2.205 lb	1 lb = 0.454 kg
gram (g) = 1,000 mg	1 g = 0.035 oz	1 oz = 28.349 g
milligram (mg) = 0.001 g		
microgram (µg) = 0.000 001 g		

Temperature Scales

Temperature can be expressed using three different scales: Fahrenheit, Celsius, and Kelvin. The SI unit for temperature is the kelvin (K).

Although 0 K is much colder than 0°C, a change of 1 K is equal to a change of 1°C.

Three Temperature Scales

	Fahrenheit	Celsius	Kelvin
Water boils	212°	100°	373
Body temperature	98.6°	37°	310
Room temperature	68°	20°	293
Water freezes	32°	0°	273

Temperature Conversions Table

To convert	Use this equation:	Example
Celsius to Fahrenheit °C ⟶ °F	$°F = \left(\dfrac{9}{5} \times °C\right) + 32$	Convert 45°C to °F. $°F = \left(\dfrac{9}{5} \times 45°C\right) + 32 = 113°F$
Fahrenheit to Celsius °F ⟶ °C	$°C = \dfrac{5}{9} \times (°F - 32)$	Convert 68°F to °C. $°C = \dfrac{5}{9} \times (68°F - 32) = 20°C$
Celsius to Kelvin °C ⟶ K	$K = °C + 273$	Convert 45°C to K. $K = 45°C + 273 = 318\ K$
Kelvin to Celsius K ⟶ °C	$°C = K - 273$	Convert 32 K to °C. $°C = 32\ K - 273 = -241°C$

Measuring Skills

Using a Graduated Cylinder

When using a graduated cylinder to measure volume, keep the following procedures in mind:

1 Make sure the cylinder is on a flat, level surface.

2 Move your head so that your eye is level with the surface of the liquid.

3 Read the mark closest to the liquid level. On glass graduated cylinders, read the mark closest to the center of the curve in the liquid's surface.

Using a Meterstick or Metric Ruler

When using a meterstick or metric ruler to measure length, keep the following procedures in mind:

1 Place the ruler firmly against the object you are measuring.

2 Align one edge of the object exactly with the zero end of the ruler.

3 Look at the other edge of the object to see which of the marks on the ruler is closest to that edge. **Note:** Each small slash between the centimeters represents a millimeter, which is one-tenth of a centimeter.

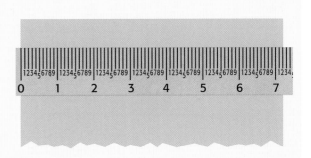

Using a Triple-Beam Balance

When using a triple-beam balance to measure mass, keep the following procedures in mind:

1 Make sure the balance is on a level surface.

2 Place all of the countermasses at zero. Adjust the balancing knob until the pointer rests at zero.

3 Place the object you wish to measure on the pan. **Caution:** Do not place hot objects or chemicals directly on the balance pan.

4 Move the largest countermass along the beam to the right until it is at the last notch that does not tip the balance. Follow the same procedure with the next-largest countermass. Then move the smallest countermass until the pointer rests at zero.

5 Add the readings from the three beams together to determine the mass of the object.

6 When determining the mass of crystals or powders, use a piece of filter paper. First find the mass of the paper. Then add the crystals or powder to the paper and re-measure. The actual mass of the crystals or powder is the total mass minus the mass of the paper. When finding the mass of liquids, first find the mass of the empty container. Then find the mass of the liquid and container together. The mass of the liquid is the total mass minus the mass of the container.

Scientific Method

The series of steps that scientists use to answer questions and solve problems is often called the **scientific method.** The scientific method is not a rigid procedure. Scientists may use all of the steps or just some of the steps of the scientific method. They may even repeat some of the steps. The goal of the scientific method is to come up with reliable answers and solutions.

Six Steps of the Scientific Method

Ask a Question Good questions come from careful **observations.** You make observations by using your senses to gather information. Sometimes you may use instruments, such as microscopes and telescopes, to extend the range of your senses. As you observe the natural world, you will discover that you have many more questions than answers. These questions drive the scientific method.

Questions beginning with *what, why, how,* and *when* are very important in focusing an investigation, and they often lead to a hypothesis. (You will learn what a hypothesis is in the next step.) Here is an example of a question that could lead to further investigation.

Question: How does acid rain affect plant growth?

Form a Hypothesis After you come up with a question, you need to turn the question into a **hypothesis.** A hypothesis is a clear statement of what you expect the answer to your question to be. Your hypothesis will represent your best "educated guess" based on your observations and what you already know. A good hypothesis is testable. If observations and information cannot be gathered or if an experiment cannot be designed to test your hypothesis, it is untestable, and the investigation can go no further.

Here is a hypothesis that could be formed from the question, "How does acid rain affect plant growth?"

Hypothesis: Acid rain causes plants to grow more slowly.

Notice that the hypothesis provides some specifics that lead to methods of testing. The hypothesis can also lead to predictions. A **prediction** is what you think will be the outcome of your experiment or data collection. Predictions are usually stated in an "if . . . then" format. For example, **if** meat is kept at room temperature, **then** it will spoil faster than meat kept in the refrigerator. More than one prediction can be made for a single hypothesis. Here is a sample prediction for the hypothesis that acid rain causes plants to grow more slowly.

Prediction: If a plant is watered with only acid rain (which has a pH of 4), then the plant will grow at half its normal rate.

3 **Test the Hypothesis** After you have formed a hypothesis and made a prediction, you should test your hypothesis. There are different ways to do this. Perhaps the most familiar way is to conduct a **controlled experiment.** A controlled experiment tests only one factor at a time. A controlled experiment has a **control group** and one or more **experimental groups.** All the factors for the control and experimental groups are the same except for one factor, which is called the **variable.** By changing only one factor, you can see the results of just that one change.

Sometimes, the nature of an investigation makes a controlled experiment impossible. For example, dinosaurs have been extinct for millions of years, and the Earth's core is surrounded by thousands of meters of rock. It would be difficult, if not impossible, to conduct controlled experiments on such things. Under such circumstances, a hypothesis may be tested by making detailed observations. Taking measurements is one way of making observations.

4 **Analyze the Results** After you have completed your experiments, made your observations, and collected your data, you must analyze all the information you have gathered. Tables and graphs are often used in this step to organize the data.

5 **Draw Conclusions** Based on the analysis of your data, you should conclude whether or not your results support your hypothesis. If your hypothesis is supported, you (or others) might want to repeat the observations or experiments to verify your results. If your hypothesis is not supported by the data, you may have to check your procedure for errors. You may even have to reject your hypothesis and make a new one. If you cannot draw a conclusion from your results, you may have to try the investigation again or carry out further observations or experiments.

Draw Conclusions

Do they support your hypothesis?

No

Yes

6 **Communicate Results** After any scientific investigation, you should report your results. By doing a written or oral report, you let others know what you have learned. They may want to repeat your investigation to see if they get the same results. Your report may even lead to another question, which in turn may lead to another investigation.

Scientific Method in Action

The scientific method is not a "straight line" of steps. It contains loops in which several steps may be repeated over and over again, while others may not be necessary. For example, sometimes scientists will find that testing one hypothesis raises new questions and new hypotheses to be tested. And sometimes, testing the hypothesis leads directly to a conclusion. Furthermore, the steps in the scientific method are not always used in the same order. Follow the steps in the diagram below, and see how many different directions the scientific method can take you.

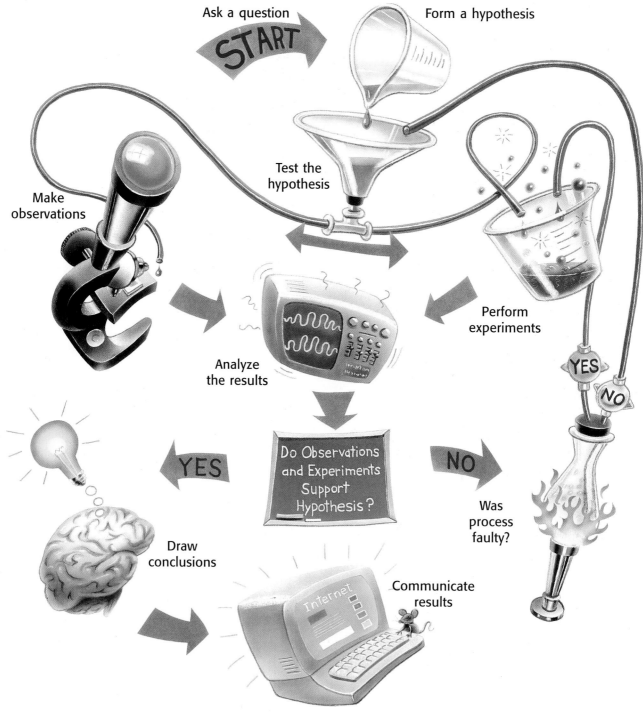

Ask a question

START

Form a hypothesis

Make observations

Test the hypothesis

Perform experiments

Analyze the results

YES

NO

YES

Do Observations and Experiments Support Hypothesis?

NO

Draw conclusions

Was process faulty?

Communicate results

Internet

Making Charts and Graphs

Circle Graphs

A circle graph, or pie chart, shows how each group of data relates to all of the data. Each part of the circle represents a category of the data. The entire circle represents all of the data. For example, a biologist studying a hardwood forest in Wisconsin found that there were five different types of trees. The data table at right summarizes the biologist's findings.

Wisconsin Hardwood Trees	
Type of tree	**Number found**
Oak	600
Maple	750
Beech	300
Birch	1,200
Hickory	150
Total	3,000

How to Make a Circle Graph

1 In order to make a circle graph of this data, first find the percentage of each type of tree. To do this, divide the number of individual trees by the total number of trees and multiply by 100.

$$\frac{600 \text{ oak}}{3,000 \text{ trees}} \times 100 = 20\%$$

$$\frac{750 \text{ maple}}{3,000 \text{ trees}} \times 100 = 25\%$$

$$\frac{300 \text{ beech}}{3,000 \text{ trees}} \times 100 = 10\%$$

$$\frac{1,200 \text{ birch}}{3,000 \text{ trees}} \times 100 = 40\%$$

$$\frac{150 \text{ hickory}}{3,000 \text{ trees}} \times 100 = 5\%$$

2 Now determine the size of the pie shapes that make up the chart. Do this by multiplying each percentage by 360°. Remember that a circle contains 360°.

$20\% \times 360° = 72°$ $25\% \times 360° = 90°$
$10\% \times 360° = 36°$ $40\% \times 360° = 144°$
$5\% \times 360° = 18°$

3 Then check that the sum of the percentages is 100 and the sum of the degrees is 360.

$20\% + 25\% + 10\% + 40\% + 5\% = 100\%$
$72° + 90° + 36° + 144° + 18° = 360°$

4 Use a compass to draw a circle and mark its center.

5 Then use a protractor to draw angles of 72°, 90°, 36°, 144°, and 18° in the circle.

6 Finally, label each part of the graph, and choose an appropriate title.

A Community of Wisconsin Hardwood Trees

Hickory 150
Oak 600
Birch 1,200
Maple 750
Beech 300

Line Graphs

Line graphs are most often used to demonstrate continuous change. For example, Mr. Smith's science class analyzed the population records for their hometown, Appleton, between 1900 and 2000. Examine the data at left.

Because the year and the population change, they are the *variables*. The population is determined by, or dependent on, the year. Therefore, the population is called the **dependent variable**, and the year is called the **independent variable**. Each set of data is called a **data pair**. To prepare a line graph, data pairs must first be organized in a table like the one at left.

Population of Appleton, 1900–2000	
Year	Population
1900	1,800
1920	2,500
1940	3,200
1960	3,900
1980	4,600
2000	5,300

How to Make a Line Graph

❶ Place the independent variable along the horizontal (*x*) axis. Place the dependent variable along the vertical (*y*) axis.

❷ Label the *x*-axis "Year" and the *y*-axis "Population." Look at your largest and smallest values for the population. Determine a scale for the *y*-axis that will provide enough space to show these values. You must use the same scale for the entire length of the axis. Find an appropriate scale for the *x*-axis too.

❸ Choose reasonable starting points for each axis.

❹ Plot the data pairs as accurately as possible.

❺ Choose a title that accurately represents the data.

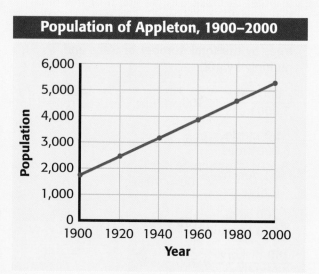

How to Determine Slope

Slope is the ratio of the change in the *y*-axis to the change in the *x*-axis, or "rise over run."

❶ Choose two points on the line graph. For example, the population of Appleton in 2000 was 5,300 people. Therefore, you can define point *a* as (2000, 5,300). In 1900, the population was 1,800 people. Define point *b* as (1900, 1,800).

❷ Find the change in the *y*-axis.
(*y* at point *a*) − (*y* at point *b*)
5,300 people − 1,800 people = 3,500 people

❸ Find the change in the *x*-axis.
(*x* at point *a*) − (*x* at point *b*)
2000 − 1900 = 100 years

❹ Calculate the slope of the graph by dividing the change in *y* by the change in *x*.

$$slope = \frac{change\ in\ y}{change\ in\ x}$$

$$slope = \frac{3,500\ people}{100\ years}$$

$$slope = 35\ people\ per\ year$$

In this example, the population in Appleton increased by a fixed amount each year. The graph of this data is a straight line. Therefore, the relationship is **linear**. When the graph of a set of data is not a straight line, the relationship is **nonlinear**.

Using Algebra to Determine Slope

The equation in step 4 may also be arranged to be:

$$y = kx$$

where y represents the change in the y-axis, k represents the slope, and x represents the change in the x-axis.

$$\text{slope} = \frac{\text{change in } y}{\text{change in } x}$$

$$k = \frac{y}{x}$$

$$k \times x = \frac{y \times x}{x}$$

$$kx = y$$

Bar Graphs

Bar graphs are used to demonstrate change that is not continuous. These graphs can be used to indicate trends when the data are taken over a long period of time. A meteorologist gathered the precipitation records at right for Hartford, Connecticut, for April 1–15, 1996, and used a bar graph to represent the data.

Precipitation in Hartford, Connecticut April 1–15, 1996

Date	Precipitation (cm)	Date	Precipitation (cm)
April 1	0.5	April 9	0.25
April 2	1.25	April 10	0.0
April 3	0.0	April 11	1.0
April 4	0.0	April 12	0.0
April 5	0.0	April 13	0.25
April 6	0.0	April 14	0.0
April 7	0.0	April 15	6.50
April 8	1.75		

How to Make a Bar Graph

1 Use an appropriate scale and a reasonable starting point for each axis.

2 Label the axes, and plot the data.

3 Choose a title that accurately represents the data.

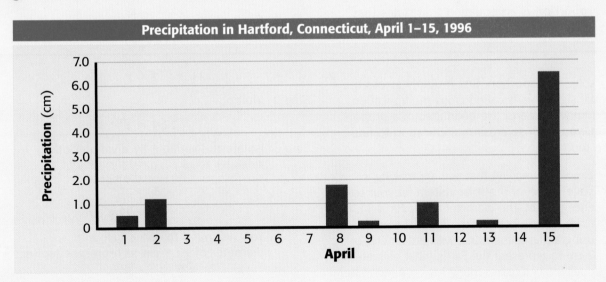

Math Refresher

Science requires an understanding of many math concepts. The following pages will help you review some important math skills.

Averages

An **average,** or **mean,** simplifies a list of numbers into a single number that *approximates* their value.

> **Example:** Find the average of the following set of numbers: 5, 4, 7, and 8.

Step 1: Find the sum.

$$5 + 4 + 7 + 8 = 24$$

Step 2: Divide the sum by the amount of numbers in your set. Because there are four numbers in this example, divide the sum by 4.

$$\frac{24}{4} = 6$$

The average, or mean, is **6.**

Ratios

A **ratio** is a comparison between numbers, and it is usually written as a fraction.

> **Example:** Find the ratio of thermometers to students if you have 36 thermometers and 48 students in your class.

Step 1: Make the ratio.

$$\frac{36 \text{ thermometers}}{48 \text{ students}}$$

Step 2: Reduce the fraction to its simplest form.

$$\frac{36}{48} = \frac{36 \div 12}{48 \div 12} = \frac{3}{4}$$

The ratio of thermometers to students is **3 to 4,** or $\frac{3}{4}$. The ratio may also be written in the form 3:4.

Proportions

A **proportion** is an equation that states that two ratios are equal.

$$\frac{3}{1} = \frac{12}{4}$$

To solve a proportion, first multiply across the equal sign. This is called cross-multiplication. If you know three of the quantities in a proportion, you can use cross-multiplication to find the fourth.

> **Example:** Imagine that you are making a scale model of the solar system for your science project. The diameter of Jupiter is 11.2 times the diameter of the Earth. If you are using a plastic-foam ball with a diameter of 2 cm to represent the Earth, what diameter does the ball representing Jupiter need to be?
>
> $$\frac{11.2}{1} = \frac{x}{2 \text{ cm}}$$

Step 1: Cross-multiply.

$$\frac{11.2}{1} \diagdown\!\!\!\!\diagup \frac{x}{2}$$

$$11.2 \times 2 = x \times 1$$

Step 2: Multiply.

$$22.4 = x \times 1$$

Step 3: Isolate the variable by dividing both sides by 1.

$$x = \frac{22.4}{1}$$

$$x = 22.4 \text{ cm}$$

You will need to use a ball with a diameter of **22.4 cm** to represent Jupiter.

Percentages

A **percentage** is a ratio of a given number to 100.

> **Example:** What is 85 percent of 40?

Step 1: Rewrite the percentage by moving the decimal point two places to the left.

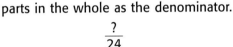

Step 2: Multiply the decimal by the number you are calculating the percentage of.

$$0.85 \times 40 = 34$$

85 percent of 40 is **34.**

Decimals

To **add** or **subtract decimals,** line up the digits vertically so that the decimal points line up. Then add or subtract the columns from right to left, carrying or borrowing numbers as necessary.

> **Example:** Add the following numbers: 3.1415 and 2.96.

Step 1: Line up the digits vertically so that the decimal points line up.

$$\begin{array}{r} 3.1415 \\ + \ 2.96 \ \ \\ \hline \end{array}$$

Step 2: Add the columns from right to left, carrying when necessary.

$$\begin{array}{r} {\scriptstyle 1\ 1} \ \ \ \ \ \\ 3.1415 \\ + \ 2.96 \ \ \\ \hline 6.1015 \end{array}$$

The sum is **6.1015.**

Fractions

Numbers tell you how many; **fractions** tell you *how much of a whole.*

> **Example:** Your class has 24 plants. Your teacher instructs you to put 5 in a shady spot. What fraction does this represent?

Step 1: Write a fraction with the total number of parts in the whole as the denominator.

$$\frac{?}{24}$$

Step 2: Write the number of parts of the whole being represented as the numerator.

$$\frac{5}{24}$$

$\frac{5}{24}$ of the plants will be in the shade.

Reducing Fractions

It is usually best to express a fraction in simplest form. This is called *reducing* a fraction.

> **Example:** Reduce the fraction $\frac{30}{45}$ to its simplest form.

Step 1: Find the largest whole number that will divide evenly into both the numerator and denominator. This number is called the greatest common factor (GCF).

factors of the numerator 30: 1, 2, 3, 5, 6, 10, **15,** 30

factors of the denominator 45: 1, 3, 5, 9, **15,** 45

Step 2: Divide both the numerator and the denominator by the GCF, which in this case is 15.

$$\frac{30}{45} = \frac{30 \div 15}{45 \div 15} = \frac{2}{3}$$

$\frac{30}{45}$ reduced to its simplest form is $\frac{2}{3}$.

Adding and Subtracting Fractions

To **add** or **subtract fractions** that have the **same denominator,** simply add or subtract the numerators.

Examples:

$$\frac{3}{5} + \frac{1}{5} = ? \quad \text{and} \quad \frac{3}{4} - \frac{1}{4} = ?$$

Step 1: Add or subtract the numerators.

$$\frac{3}{5} + \frac{1}{5} = \frac{4}{} \quad \text{and} \quad \frac{3}{4} - \frac{1}{4} = \frac{2}{}$$

Step 2: Write the sum or difference over the denominator.

$$\frac{3}{5} + \frac{1}{5} = \frac{4}{5} \quad \text{and} \quad \frac{3}{4} - \frac{1}{4} = \frac{2}{4}$$

Step 3: If necessary, reduce the fraction to its simplest form.

$$\frac{4}{5} \text{ cannot be reduced, and } \frac{2}{4} = \frac{1}{2}.$$

To **add** or **subtract fractions** that have **different denominators,** first find the least common denominator (LCD).

Examples:

$$\frac{1}{2} + \frac{1}{6} = ? \quad \text{and} \quad \frac{3}{4} - \frac{2}{3} = ?$$

Step 1: Write the equivalent fractions with a common denominator.

$$\frac{3}{6} + \frac{1}{6} = ? \quad \text{and} \quad \frac{9}{12} - \frac{8}{12} = ?$$

Step 2: Add or subtract.

$$\frac{3}{6} + \frac{1}{6} = \frac{4}{6} \quad \text{and} \quad \frac{9}{12} - \frac{8}{12} = \frac{1}{12}$$

Step 3: If necessary, reduce the fraction to its simplest form.

$$\frac{4}{6} = \frac{2}{3}, \text{ and } \frac{1}{12} \text{ cannot be reduced.}$$

Multiplying Fractions

To **multiply fractions,** multiply the numerators and the denominators together, and then reduce the fraction to its simplest form.

Example:

$$\frac{5}{9} \times \frac{7}{10} = ?$$

Step 1: Multiply the numerators and denominators.

$$\frac{5}{9} \times \frac{7}{10} = \frac{5 \times 7}{9 \times 10} = \frac{35}{90}$$

Step 2: Reduce.

$$\frac{35}{90} = \frac{35 \div 5}{90 \div 5} = \frac{7}{18}$$

Dividing Fractions

To **divide fractions,** first rewrite the divisor (the number you divide *by*) upside down. This is called the reciprocal of the divisor. Then you can multiply and reduce if necessary.

Example:

$$\frac{5}{8} \div \frac{3}{2} = ?$$

Step 1: Rewrite the divisor as its reciprocal.

$$\frac{3}{2} \rightarrow \frac{2}{3}$$

Step 2: Multiply.

$$\frac{5}{8} \times \frac{2}{3} = \frac{5 \times 2}{8 \times 3} = \frac{10}{24}$$

Step 3: Reduce.

$$\frac{10}{24} = \frac{10 \div 2}{24 \div 2} = \frac{5}{12}$$

Scientific Notation

Scientific notation is a short way of representing very large and very small numbers without writing all of the place-holding zeros.

> **Example:** Write 653,000,000 in scientific notation.

Step 1: Write the number without the place-holding zeros.

653

Step 2: Place the decimal point after the first digit.

6.53

Step 3: Find the exponent by counting the number of places that you moved the decimal point.

6₌53000000

The decimal point was moved eight places to the left. Therefore, the exponent of 10 is positive 8. Remember, if the decimal point had moved to the right, the exponent would be negative.

Step 4: Write the number in scientific notation.

$$\mathbf{6.53 \times 10^8}$$

Area

Area is the number of square units needed to cover the surface of an object.

Formulas:
Area of a square = side × side
Area of a rectangle = length × width
Area of a triangle = $\frac{1}{2}$ × base × height

Examples: Find the areas.

Triangle
Area = $\frac{1}{2}$ × base × height
Area = $\frac{1}{2}$ × 3 cm × 4 cm
Area = **6 cm²**

4 cm

3 cm

Rectangle
Area = length × width
Area = 6 cm × 3 cm
Area = **18 cm²**

3 cm

6 cm

Square
Area = side × side
Area = 3 cm × 3 cm
Area = **9 cm²**

3 cm

3 cm

Volume

Volume is the amount of space something occupies.

Formulas:
Volume of a cube = side × side × side

Volume of a prism = area of base × height

Examples:
Find the volume of the solids.

Cube
Volume = side × side × side
Volume = 4 cm × 4 cm × 4 cm
Volume = **64 cm³**

4 cm
4 cm
4 cm

Prism
Volume = area of base × height
Volume = (area of triangle) × height
Volume = $\left(\frac{1}{2} \times 3 \text{ cm} \times 4 \text{ cm} \right)$ × 5 cm
Volume = 6 cm² × 5 cm
Volume = **30 cm³**

4 cm
3 cm
5 cm

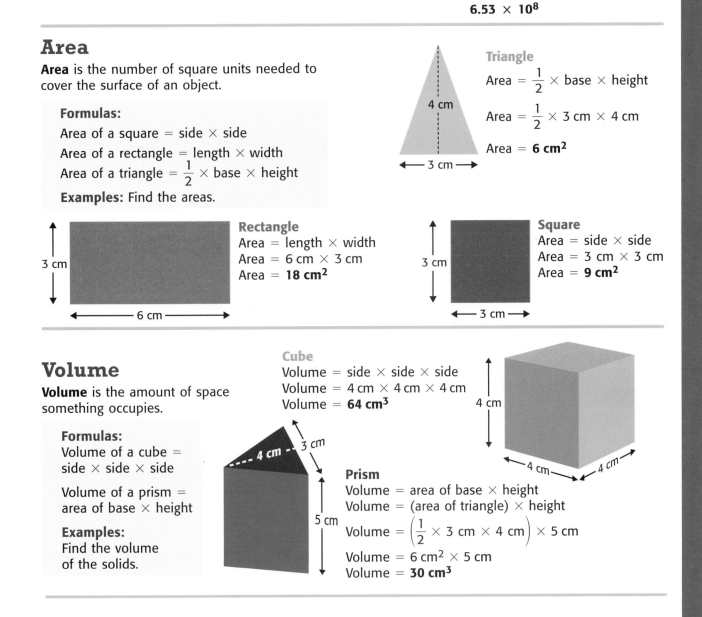

Periodic Table of the Elements

Each square on the table includes an element's name, chemical symbol, atomic number, and atomic mass.

Atomic number ——— 6

Chemical symbol ——— **C**

Element name ——— Carbon

Atomic mass ——— 12.0

The background color indicates the type of element. Carbon is a nonmetal.

The color of the chemical symbol indicates the physical state at room temperature. Carbon is a solid.

Background

Metals

Metalloids

Nonmetals

Chemical Symbol

Solid

Liquid

Gas

Period 1

1
H
Hydrogen
1.0

	Group 1	Group 2
Period 2	3 **Li** Lithium 6.9	4 **Be** Beryllium 9.0
Period 3	11 **Na** Sodium 23.0	12 **Mg** Magnesium 24.3

	Group 1	Group 2	Group 3	Group 4	Group 5	Group 6	Group 7	Group 8	Group 9
Period 4	19 **K** Potassium 39.1	20 **Ca** Calcium 40.1	21 **Sc** Scandium 45.0	22 **Ti** Titanium 47.9	23 **V** Vanadium 50.9	24 **Cr** Chromium 52.0	25 **Mn** Manganese 54.9	26 **Fe** Iron 55.8	27 **Co** Cobalt 58.9
Period 5	37 **Rb** Rubidium 85.5	38 **Sr** Strontium 87.6	39 **Y** Yttrium 88.9	40 **Zr** Zirconium 91.2	41 **Nb** Niobium 92.9	42 **Mo** Molybdenum 95.9	43 **Tc** Technetium (97.9)	44 **Ru** Ruthenium 101.1	45 **Rh** Rhodium 102.9
Period 6	55 **Cs** Cesium 132.9	56 **Ba** Barium 137.3	57 **La** Lanthanum 138.9	72 **Hf** Hafnium 178.5	73 **Ta** Tantalum 180.9	74 **W** Tungsten 183.8	75 **Re** Rhenium 186.2	76 **Os** Osmium 190.2	77 **Ir** Iridium 192.2
Period 7	87 **Fr** Francium (223.0)	88 **Ra** Radium (226.0)	89 **Ac** Actinium (227.0)	104 **Rf** Rutherfordium (261.1)	105 **Db** Dubnium (262.1)	106 **Sg** Seaborgium (263.1)	107 **Bh** Bohrium (262.1)	108 **Hs** Hassium (265)	109 **Mt** Meitnerium (266)

A row of elements is called a period.

A column of elements is called a group or family.

Lanthanides	58 **Ce** Cerium 140.1	59 **Pr** Praseodymium 140.9	60 **Nd** Neodymium 144.2	61 **Pm** Promethium (144.9)	62 **Sm** Samarium 150.4
Actinides	90 **Th** Thorium 232.0	91 **Pa** Protactinium 231.0	92 **U** Uranium 238.0	93 **Np** Neptunium (237.0)	94 **Pu** Plutonium 244.1

These elements are placed below the table to allow the table to be narrower.

This zigzag line reminds you where the metals, nonmetals, and metalloids are.

Group 18

2
He
Helium
4.0

Group 13	Group 14	Group 15	Group 16	Group 17	
5 **B** Boron 10.8	6 **C** Carbon 12.0	7 **N** Nitrogen 14.0	8 **O** Oxygen 16.0	9 **F** Fluorine 19.0	10 **Ne** Neon 20.2
13 **Al** Aluminum 27.0	14 **Si** Silicon 28.1	15 **P** Phosphorus 31.0	16 **S** Sulfur 32.1	17 **Cl** Chlorine 35.5	18 **Ar** Argon 39.9

Group 10	Group 11	Group 12						
28 **Ni** Nickel 58.7	29 **Cu** Copper 63.5	30 **Zn** Zinc 65.4	31 **Ga** Gallium 69.7	32 **Ge** Germanium 72.6	33 **As** Arsenic 74.9	34 **Se** Selenium 79.0	35 **Br** Bromine 79.9	36 **Kr** Krypton 83.8
46 **Pd** Palladium 106.4	47 **Ag** Silver 107.9	48 **Cd** Cadmium 112.4	49 **In** Indium 114.8	50 **Sn** Tin 118.7	51 **Sb** Antimony 121.8	52 **Te** Tellurium 127.6	53 **I** Iodine 126.9	54 **Xe** Xenon 131.3
78 **Pt** Platinum 195.1	79 **Au** Gold 197.0	80 **Hg** Mercury 200.6	81 **Tl** Thallium 204.4	82 **Pb** Lead 207.2	83 **Bi** Bismuth 209.0	84 **Po** Polonium (209.0)	85 **At** Astatine (210.0)	86 **Rn** Radon (222.0)
110 **Uun*** Ununnilium (271)	111 **Uuu*** Unununium (272)	112 **Uub*** Ununbium (277)		114 **Uuq*** Ununquadium (285)		116 **Uuh*** Ununhexium (289)		118 **Uuo*** Ununoctium (293)

A number in parenthesis is the mass number of the most stable form of that element.

63 **Eu** Europium 152.0	64 **Gd** Gadolinium 157.3	65 **Tb** Terbium 158.9	66 **Dy** Dysprosium 162.5	67 **Ho** Holmium 164.9	68 **Er** Erbium 167.3	69 **Tm** Thulium 168.9	70 **Yb** Ytterbium 173.0	71 **Lu** Lutetium 175.0
95 **Am** Americium (243.1)	96 **Cm** Curium (247.1)	97 **Bk** Berkelium (247.1)	98 **Cf** Californium (251.1)	99 **Es** Einsteinium (252.1)	100 **Fm** Fermium (257.1)	101 **Md** Mendelevium (258.1)	102 **No** Nobelium (259.1)	103 **Lr** Lawrencium (262.1)

*The official names and symbols for the elements greater than 109 will eventually be approved by a committee of scientists.

The Six Kingdoms

Kingdom Archaebacteria

The organisms in this kingdom are single-celled prokaryotes.

Archaebacteria		
Group	**Examples**	**Characteristics**
Methanogens	*Methanococcus*	found in soil, swamps, the digestive tract of mammals; produce methane gas; can't live in oxygen
Thermophiles	*Sulpholobus*	found in extremely hot environments; require sulphur, can't live in oxygen
Halophiles	*Halococcus*	found in environments with very high salt content, such as the Dead Sea; nearly all can live in oxygen

Kingdom Eubacteria

There are more than 4,000 named species in this kingdom of single-celled prokaryotes.

Eubacteria		
Group	**Examples**	**Characteristics**
Bacilli	*Escherichia coli*	rod-shaped; free-living, symbiotic, or parasitic; some can fix nitrogen; some cause disease
Cocci	*Streptococcus*	spherical-shaped, disease-causing; can form spores to resist unfavorable environments
Spirilla	*Treponema*	spiral-shaped; responsible for several serious illnesses, such as syphilis and Lyme disease

Kingdom Protista

The organisms in this kingdom are eukaryotes. There are single-celled and multicellular representatives.

Protists		
Group	**Examples**	**Characteristics**
Sacodines	*Amoeba*	radiolarians; single-celled consumers
Ciliates	*Paramecium*	single-celled consumers
Flagellates	*Trypanosoma*	single-celled parasites
Sporozoans	*Plasmodium*	single-celled parasites
Euglenas	*Euglena*	single-celled; photosynthesize
Diatoms	*Pinnularia*	most are single-celled; photosynthesize
Dinoflagellates	*Gymnodinium*	single-celled; some photosynthesize
Algae	*Volvox*, coral algae	4 phyla; single- or many-celled; photosynthesize
Slime molds	*Physarum*	single- or many-celled; consumers or decomposers
Water molds	powdery mildew	single- or many-celled, parasites or decomposers

Kingdom Fungi

There are single-celled and multicellular eukaryotes in this kingdom. There are four major groups of fungi.

Fungi		
Group	**Examples**	**Characteristics**
Threadlike fungi	bread mold	spherical; decomposers
Sac fungi	yeast, morels	saclike; parasites and decomposers
Club fungi	mushrooms, rusts, smuts	club-shaped; parasites and decomposers
Lichens	British soldier	symbiotic with algae

Kingdom Plantae

The organisms in this kingdom are multicellular eukaryotes. They have specialized organ systems for different life processes. They are classified in divisions instead of phyla.

Plants		
Group	**Examples**	**Characteristics**
Bryophytes	mosses, liverworts	reproduce by spores
Club mosses	*Lycopodium,* ground pine	reproduce by spores
Horsetails	rushes	reproduce by spores
Ferns	spleenworts, sensitive fern	reproduce by spores
Conifers	pines, spruces, firs	reproduce by seeds; cones
Cycads	*Zamia*	reproduce by seeds
Gnetophytes	*Welwitschia*	reproduce by seeds
Ginkgoes	*Ginkgo*	reproduce by seeds
Angiosperms	all flowering plants	reproduce by seeds; flowers

Kingdom Animalia

This kingdom contains multicellular eukaryotes. They have specialized tissues and complex organ systems.

Animals		
Group	**Examples**	**Characteristics**
Sponges	glass sponges	no symmetry or segmentation; aquatic
Cnidarians	jellyfish, coral	radial symmetry; aquatic
Flatworms	planaria, tapeworms, flukes	bilateral symmetry; organ systems
Roundworms	*Trichina,* hookworms	bilateral symmetry; organ systems
Annelids	earthworms, leeches	bilateral symmetry; organ systems
Mollusks	snails, octopuses	bilateral symmetry; organ systems
Echinoderms	sea stars, sand dollars	radial symmetry; organ systems
Arthropods	insects, spiders, lobsters	bilateral symmetry; organ systems
Chordates	fish, amphibians, reptiles, birds, mammals	bilateral symmetry; complex organ systems

Using the Microscope

Parts of the Compound Light Microscope

- The **ocular lens** magnifies the image 10×.

- The **low-power objective** magnifies the image 10×.

- The **high-power objective** magnifies the image either 40× or 43×.

- The **revolving nosepiece** holds the objectives and can be turned to change from one magnification to the other.

- The **body tube** maintains the correct distance between the ocular lens and objectives.

- The **coarse-adjustment knob** moves the body tube up and down to allow focusing of the image.

- The **fine-adjustment knob** moves the body tube slightly to bring the image into sharper focus.

- The **stage** supports a slide.

- **Stage clips** hold the slide in place for viewing.

- The **diaphragm** controls the amount of light coming through the stage.

- The light source provides a **light** for viewing the slide.

- The **arm** supports the body tube.

- The **base** supports the microscope.

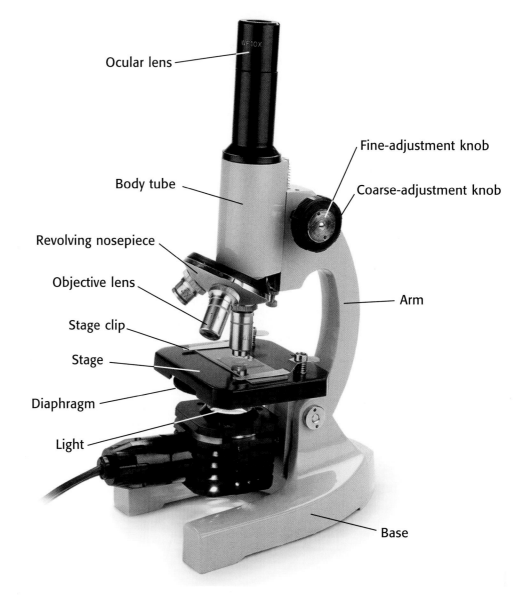

Ocular lens

Fine-adjustment knob

Body tube

Coarse-adjustment knob

Revolving nosepiece

Objective lens

Arm

Stage clip

Stage

Diaphragm

Light

Base

Proper Use of the Compound Light Microscope

1 Carry the microscope to your lab table using both hands. Place one hand beneath the base, and use the other hand to hold the arm of the microscope. Hold the microscope close to your body while moving it to your lab table.

2 Place the microscope on the lab table at least 5 cm from the edge of the table.

3 Check to see what type of light source is used by your microscope. If the microscope has a lamp, plug it in, making sure that the cord is out of the way. If the microscope has a mirror, adjust it to reflect light through the hole in the stage.
Caution: If your microscope has a mirror, do not use direct sunlight as a light source. Direct sunlight can damage your eyes.

4 Always begin work with the low-power objective in line with the body tube. Adjust the revolving nosepiece.

5 Place a prepared slide over the hole in the stage. Secure the slide with the stage clips.

6 Look through the ocular lens. Move the diaphragm to adjust the amount of light coming through the stage.

7 Look at the stage from eye level. Slowly turn the coarse adjustment to lower the objective until it almost touches the slide. Do not allow the objective to touch the slide.

8 Look through the ocular lens. Turn the coarse adjustment to raise the low-power objective until the image is in focus. Always focus by raising the objective away from the slide. *Never focus the objective downward.* Use the fine adjustment to sharpen the focus. Keep both eyes open while viewing a slide.

9 Make sure that the image is exactly in the center of your field of vision. Then switch to the high-power objective. Focus the image, using only the fine adjustment. *Never use the coarse adjustment at high power.*

10 When you are finished using the microscope, remove the slide. Clean the ocular lens and objective lenses with lens paper. Return the microscope to its storage area. Remember, you should use both hands to carry the microscope.

Making a Wet Mount

1 Use lens paper to clean a glass slide and a coverslip.

2 Place the specimen you wish to observe in the center of the slide.

3 Using a medicine dropper, place one drop of water on the specimen.

4 Hold the coverslip at the edge of the water and at a 45° angle to the slide. Make sure that the water runs along the edge of the coverslip.

5 Lower the coverslip slowly to avoid trapping air bubbles.

6 Water might evaporate from the slide as you work. Add more water to keep the specimen fresh. Place the tip of the medicine dropper next to the edge of the coverslip. Add a drop of water. (You can also use this method to add stain or solutions to a wet mount.) Remove excess water from the slide by using the corner of a paper towel as a blotter. Do not lift the coverslip to add or remove water.

Glossary

A

algae   (AL jee) protists that convert the sun's energy into food through photosynthesis (48)

angiosperm   (AN jee oh SPUHRM) a plant that produces seeds in flowers (77)

Animalia   the classification kingdom containing complex, multicellular organisms that lack cell walls, are usually able to move around, and possess nervous systems that help them be aware of and react to their surroundings (157)

antibiotic   a substance used to kill or slow the growth of bacteria or other microorganisms (30)

Archaebacteria   (AHR kee bak TIR ee uh) a classification kingdom containing bacteria that thrive in extreme environments (24, 28)

asexual reproduction   reproduction in which a single parent produces offspring that are genetically identical to the parent (6)

ATP   adenosine triphosphate; the molecule that provides energy for a cell's activities (13)

B

bacteria   extremely small, single-celled organisms without a nucleus; prokaryotic cells (24)

binary fission   the simple cell division in which one cell splits into two; used by bacteria (25)

bioremediation   (BIE oh ri MEE dee AY shun) the use of bacteria and other microorganisms to change pollutants in soil and water into harmless chemicals (30)

budding   a type of asexual reproduction in which a small part of the parent's body develops into an independent organism (60)

C

carbohydrate   a biochemical composed of one or more simple sugars bonded together that is used to provide and store energy (11)

cell   a membrane-covered structure that contains all of the materials necessary for life (4)

cell membrane   a phospholipid layer that covers a cell's surface and acts as a barrier between the inside of a cell and the cell's environment (12)

cell wall   a structure that surrounds the cell membrane of some cells and provides strength and support to the cell membrane (75)

cellular respiration   the process of producing ATP in the cell from oxygen and glucose; releases carbon dioxide and water (111)

chlorophyll   a green pigment in chloroplasts that absorbs light energy for photosynthesis (74, 110)

chloroplast   an organelle found in plant and algae cells where photosynthesis occurs (51)

club fungus   a type of fungus characterized by umbrella-shaped mushrooms (61)

consumer   an organism that eats producers or other organisms for energy (8, 27)

controlled experiment   an experiment that tests only one factor at a time (145)

cotyledon   (KAHT uh LEED uhn) a seed leaf inside a seed (87)

cuticle   a waxy layer that coats the surface of stems, leaves, and other plant parts exposed to air (74)

D

deciduous   describes trees with leaves that change color in autumn and fall off in winter (116)

decomposer   an organism that gets energy by breaking down the remains of dead organisms or animal wastes and consuming or absorbing the nutrients (8)

DNA   deoxyribonucleic (dee AHKS ee RIE boh noo KLEE ik) acid; hereditary material that controls all the activities of a cell, contains the information to make new cells, and provides instructions for making proteins (6)

dormant   describes an inactive state of a seed (108)

E

endospore   a bacterium surrounded by a thick, protective membrane (25)

enzyme   a protein that makes it possible for certain chemical reactions to occur quickly (10)

epidermis   the outermost layer of cells covering roots, stems, leaves, and flower parts (89)

Eubacteria   (YOO bak TIR ee uh) a classification kingdom containing mostly free-living bacteria found in many varied environments (27)

eukaryotic cell (eukaryote)   (yoo KER ee OHT) a cell that contains a central nucleus and a complicated internal structure (46)

evergreen   describes trees that keep their leaves year-round (116)

F

fibrous root   a type of root in which there are several roots of the same size that spread out from the base of the stem (89)

Fungi   a kingdom of complex organisms that obtain food by breaking down other substances in their surroundings and absorbing the nutrients (57)

fungus an organism in the kingdom Fungi (57)

funguslike protist a protist that obtains its food from dead organic matter or from the body of another organism (47)

G

gametophyte (guh MEET oh FIET) a stage in a plant life cycle during which eggs and sperm are produced (75)

gravitropism (GRAV i TROH PIZ uhm) a change in the growth of a plant in response to gravity (114)

gymnosperm (JIM noh SPUHRM) a plant that produces seeds but not flowers (77)

H

hemoglobin (HEE moh GLOH bin) the protein in red blood cells that attaches to oxygen so that oxygen can be carried through the body (10)

heredity the passing of traits from parent to offspring (6)

homeostasis (HOH mee OH STAY sis) the maintenance of a stable internal environment (5)

host an organism on which a parasite lives (33, 48)

hyphae (HIE fee) chains of cells that make up multicellular fungi (58)

hypothesis a possible explanation or answer to a question (144)

I

imperfect fungus a fungus that does not fit into other standard groups of fungi (62)

K

kingdom the most general of the seven levels of classification (156)

L

lactic-acid bacteria bacteria that digest the milk sugar lactose and convert it into lactic acid (31)

lichen the combination of a fungus and an alga that grows intertwined and exists in a symbiotic relationship (63)

lipid a type of biochemical, including fats and oils, that does not dissolve in water; lipids store energy and make up cell membranes (12)

M

mass the amount of matter that something is made of; its value does not change with the object's location (141)

metabolism (muh TAB uh LIZ uhm) the combined chemical processes that occur in a cell or living organism (6)

meter the basic unit of length in the SI system (141)

mold shapeless, fuzzy fungi (59)

mycelium (mie SEE lee uhm) a twisted mass of fungal hyphae that have grown together (58)

N

nitrogen cycle the movement of nitrogen from the nonliving environment into living organisms and back again (29)

nitrogen fixation the process of changing nitrogen gas into forms that plants can use (29)

nonvascular plant a plant that depends on the processes of diffusion and osmosis to move materials from one part of the plant to another (76)

nucleic acid a biochemical that stores information needed to build proteins and other nucleic acids; made up of subunits called nucleotides (13)

nucleotide a subunit of DNA consisting of a sugar, a phosphate, and one of four nitrogenous bases (13)

O

ovary in flowers, the structure containing ovules that will develop into fruit following fertilization (95)

P

parasite an organism that feeds on another living creature, usually without killing it (48)

pathogenic bacteria bacteria that invade a host organism and obtain the nutrients they need from the host's cells (32)

petals the often colorful structures on a flower that are usually involved in attracting pollinators (94)

phloem (FLOH EM) a specialized plant tissue that transports sugar molecules from one part of the plant to another (88)

phospholipid a type of lipid molecule that forms much of a cell's membrane (12)

photosynthesis (FOHT oh SIN thuh sis) the process by which plants capture light energy from the sun and convert it into sugar (74)

phototropism a change in the growth of a plant in response to light (113)

phytoplankton (FITE oh PLANK tuhn) a microscopic photosynthetic organism that floats near the surface of the ocean (19)

pistils the female reproductive structures in a flower that consist of a stigma, a style, and an ovary (95)

Plantae the kingdom that contains plants—complex, multicellular organisms that are usually green and use the sun's energy to make sugar by photosynthesis (157)

GLOSSARY

pollen the dustlike particles that carry the male gametophyte of seed plants (82)

pollination the transfer of pollen to the female cone in conifers or to the stigma in angiosperms (85)

producer organisms that make their own food, usually by using the energy from sunlight to make sugar (8, 27)

prokaryotic cell (prokaryote) (proh KER ee OHT) a cell that does not have a nucleus or any other membrane-covered organelles; also called a bacterium (24)

protein a biochemical that is composed of amino acids; its functions include regulating chemical reactions, transporting and storing materials, and providing support (10)

protist an organism that belongs to the kingdom Protista (46)

Protista a kingdom of eukaryotic single-celled or simple, multicellular organisms; kingdom Protista contains all eukaryotes that are not plants, animals, or fungi (46, 156)

protozoa animal-like protists that are single-celled consumers (52)

pseudopodia (SOO doh POH dee uh) structures that amoebas use to move around (52)

R

rhizoids small, hairlike threads of cells that help hold nonvascular plants in place (78)

rhizome the underground stem of a fern (80)

S

sac fungus a type of fungus that reproduces using spores, which develop in a sac called an ascus (60)

scientific method a series of steps that scientists use to answer questions and solve problems (144)

sepals the leaflike structures that cover and protect an immature flower (94)

sexual reproduction reproduction in which two sex cells join to form a zygote; sexual reproduction produces offspring that share characteristics of both parents (6)

spore a small reproductive cell protected by a thick wall (58)

sporophyte (SPOH roh FIET) a stage in a plant life cycle during which spores are produced (75)

stamen the male reproductive structure in a flower that consists of a filament topped by a pollen-producing anther (95)

stigma the flower part that is located at the tip of the pistil (95)

stimulus anything that affects the activity of an organism, organ, or tissue (5, 113)

stomata openings in the epidermis and cuticle of a leaf that allow carbon dioxide to enter the leaf (93, 112)

symbiosis (SIM bie OH sis) a close, long-term association between two or more species (53)

T

taproot a type of root that consists of one main root that grows downward, with many smaller branch roots coming out of it (89)

threadlike fungus a fungus that develops from a spore called a zygospore (59)

transpiration the loss of water from plant leaves through openings called stomata (112)

tropism a change in the growth of a plant in response to a stimulus (113)

V

variable a factor in a controlled experiment that changes (145)

vascular plant a plant that has specialized tissues called xylem and phloem, which move materials from one part of the plant to another (77)

virus a microscopic particle that invades a cell and often destroys it (33)

volume the amount of space that something occupies or the amount of space that something contains (153)

X

xylem (ZIE luhm) a specialized plant tissue that transports water and minerals from one part of the plant to another (88)

Index

Boldface numbers refer to an illustration on that page.

A

AIDS (acquired immune deficiency syndrome), 33
air
    composition of, 9
    pollution, 63
algae, 48–51, **48–51**, 76, **76**
    in lichens, 63, **63**
    multicellular, 48, **48**
    single-celled, **48**, 49
    types of, 49–50
amber, 25, **25**
amebic dysentery, 52
amino acids, 10
amoeba, 52–53, **52–53**, 56
angiosperms, 77, **77**, 82, 86–87
    monocots and dicots, 87, **87**
animal-like protists, 52–55, **52–55**
animals
    pollination by, 86, **86**
anther, **94,** 95
antibiotic-resistant microorganisms, 43
antibiotics, 43
    produced by bacteria, 30
    produced by fungi, 60, 62, **62**
    treatment of bacterial disease with, 30
archaebacteria, 24, 28, **28**
ascus, 60
asexual reproduction, 6, **6**, 56, **56**, 58, 109, **109**
athlete's foot 62
atoms, 10
ATP (adenosine triphosphate), 13, **13**

B

bacilli, 26
bacteria, 24–28
    antibiotic resistance in, 43
    classification of, 24, 27–28
    in environment, 24
    in food production, 31, **31**
    genetically engineered, 30–31, **30**
    in nitrogen cycle, 29, **29**
    obtaining nutrients, 27, **27**
    pathogens, 32, **32,** 43
    reproduction in, 25, **25**
    role in environment, 29–30, **29–30**
    shape of, 26
    size of, 24, **24**
bacterial infection, 32, **32**
    treatment of, 43

bacteriophage, 43
bar graphs, 149, **149**
basidia, 61
bear, **6**
bees, 86, **86**
binary fission, 25, **25**
bioremediation, 30, **30**
birds, nests of, **57**
blood-sugar level, 5
body temperature, regulation of, 5
bracket fungi, 62, **62**
brown algae, 49, **49**
bubonic plague, 32, **32**
budding, **6**
    in yeast, 60, **60**

C

cactus, 87, **90**, 93
carbohydrates, 11, **11**
    complex, 11, **11**
    energy in, 13, **13**
    simple, 11, **11**
carbon dioxide
    diffusion into leaf, 112, **112**
    photosynthesis and, 9, 111, **111**
careers, ethnobotanist, 103
cell, 4, **4,** 10–13, **12–13**
    specialized, 4
cell membrane, 4, 12, **12**
cell wall, 75, **75**
    of archaebacteria, 28
    of fungi, 70
cellular respiration, 111
cheese production, 31, **31,** 62
Chlamydomonas, 48
chlorophyll, 27, 48–49, 74, 110, **110**, 117, **117**
chloroplast, **51**, 74, 110
chrysanthemum, 115
cilia, of ciliates, 54, **54**
ciliates, 54, **54**
citric acid, 62
club fungi, 61–62, **61**
club mosses, 77, **77**, 79, **79**, 81, **81**
cocci, 26
colony, *Volvox*, 49, **49**
common cold, 33
cones (plant), **84–85**, 85
conifer, 84–85, **84–85**
conjugation, 56, **56**
consumers, 8, **8**, 27
    fungi, 57
    protists, 46
    slime molds, 47, **47**
contractile vacuole, **51**, 52, 54
cotyledon, 87, **87**
cuticle (plant), 74, **93**, 112, **112**
cyanobacteria, 27, **27**
cyclosporin, 70

D

deciduous, 116, **116**
decomposers, 8, **8**
    fungi, 57
    bacteria, 227, **27**, 29
    water molds, 48
dental cavities, 32
development
    as a characteristic of living things, 7, **7**
    of fruit, 107, **107**
    of seeds, 107, **107**
diabetes mellitus, 31
diatoms, 50, **50**
dicots, 87, **87**, 89
dinoflagellates, 50, **50**
DNA (deoxyribonucleic acid), 6, 13
drugs, from fungi, 70

E

element, 10
endospore, 25, **25**
energy
    in ATP, 13, **13**
    use by living things, 6
environment
    plant responses to, 113–117, **113–117**
enzymes, 10
epidermis
    of leaf, 93, **93**
    of root, 89
Escherichia coli, 30–31
eubacteria, 24, 27, **27**
Euglena, 56, **56**
euglenoids, 51, **51**
eukaryotes, protists, 46–56
evergreen, 116
evolution, of plants, 27, 76, **76**
eyespots, **51**

F

fairy rings, **61**
fat, 12
feathers, **10**
feeding
    in amoebas, 52, **52**
    in ciliates, 54, **54**
ferns, 74, **74**, 77, 79–81, **79–80**
    importance of, 81
    life cycle of, 80, **80**
fertilization
    in plants, 75, **75**, 106, **106**
fibroblasts, 70
fibrous root, 89, **89**
filament, of stamen, **94**, 95
fir tree, 82, 84

fission, 56, **56**
flagella
    of bacteria, 26
    of dinoflagellates, 50
    of euglenoids, **51**
    of flagellates, 53, **53**
flagellates, 53, **53**
Fleming, Alexander, 30, 43
flower, 86–87, **87**, 94–95, **94–95,**
    115, **115**
flowering plants. *See* angiosperms
flu, 33
food
    as a necessity of life, 8
    bacteria in production of 231, **31**
food crops, 87
food poisoning, 32
food reserves, seeds, 83, **83**
food vacuole, 52, **54**
foraminiferans, 53
fossil fuel, 81
frond, 80, **80**
fruit, 82, 86, 95
    development of, 107, **107**
    dispersal of, 86, **86**
fungus, 57–69
    bandages from, 70
    cell walls of, 70
    characteristics of, 57–58
    food for, 57
    hyphae and mycelium of, 58, **58**
    kinds of, 59–63, **59–63**
    in lichens, 63, **63**
    reproduction in, 58
funguslike protists, 47–48, **47–48**

G

gametophyte, 75, **75**, 82
gas exchange, in plants, 112, **112**
genetic engineering, of bacteria,
    30–31, **30**
germination, of seeds, 83, 108, **108**
Giardia lamblia, 53, **53**
gills, of mushrooms, 61
glucose, photosynthesis and, 111,
    111
gnetophytes, 84
grass, 86–87
gravitropism, 114, **114**
green algae, 49, **49**, 76, **76**
growth, of living things, 7, **7**
guard cells, 93, **93**, 112, **112**
gymnosperms, 77, **77**, 82, 84–85,
    84–85

H

hair, **10**
heat-loving bacteria, 28
hemoglobin, 10
herbaceous stem, 91, **91**
heredity, 6, **6**
HIV, 33–34
homeostasis, 5

horsetails, 77, **77,** 79, **79**, 81, **81**
host, 33, 48
hydra, **6**
hydrogen, 10
hyphae, 58, **58**

I

imperfect fungi, 62, **62**
influenza virus, 34
insects, pollination by, 86, **86**
insulin, 31
Irish potato famine, 48

L

lactic acid bacteria, 31
Laminaria, 49
leaf, 92–93, **92–93**
    adaptations of, 93, **93**
    functions of, 92
    seasonal changes in, 116–117,
        116–117
    structure of, 93, **93**
lichen, 63, **63**
light
    in photosynthesis, 110–111, **111**
lipids, 12, **12**
    energy in, **13**
liverworts, 76, **76–77**, 78–79, **79**, 81
living things, 4–7
    cells of, 4, **4**
    chemistry of, 10–13
    necessities of, 8–9, **8–9**
    use of energy, 6
long-day plants, 115
Lyme disease, 32
lysogenic cycle, 35, **35**
lytic cycle, 35, **35**

M

macronucleus, 54, **54**
malaria, 55, **55**
maple tree, 86, 116, **116**
metabolism, 6
    dependence on water, 8
methane-making bacteria, 28
micronucleus, 54, **54**
mold (fungi), 59
molecule, 10
monkey, 4, **4**
monocots, 87, **87,** 89
morels, 60
mosquito, carrier of malaria, 55, **55**
mosses, 76, **76–78,** 78–79
multicellular organism, 4, **4**
muscle cells, 4
mushroom, 61–62, **61**
mycelium, 58, **58**

N

nerve cells, 4

nitrogen, 10
    in atmosphere, 29, **29**
    nitrogen cycle, 29, **29**
    nitrogen fixation, 29, **29**
nonvascular plants, 76, **76, 77**
nucleic acids, 13
nucleotides, 13

O

oak tree, **7,** 82
oil spill, 30
oils, 12
onion, 87, **89**
orchid, 87, **94**
ovary, of flower, **94–95,** 95,
    106–108, **106–108**
ovule, **94–95,** 95, 106–108,
    106–108
oxygen, 10
    photosynthesis and, 111, **111**
    release from leaves, 112, **112**

P

palisade layer, 93, **93**
Paramecium, **46,** 54, **54**
    conjugation in, 56, **56**
parasite
    amoebas, 52
    bacteria, 27
    flagellates, 53
    water molds, 48, **48**
pathogens
    bacteria, 32, **32**
    viruses, 33
penicillin, 43, 62
Penicillium, 62, **62**
percentages, 77, 151
petal, 94, **94, 106**
phloem, 88, **89,** 90, 91
phospholipids, 12, **12**
    in cell membranes, 12, **12**
photosynthesis, 9, 74, 90, 92–93,
    110–111, **110–111**
    in algae, 48
    in bacteria, 27
    capture of light energy, 110, **110**
    in protists, 46
    sugar production in, 111, **111**
phototropism, 113, **113**
phytoplankton, 49–50
pine tree, 82, 84–85, **84–85**
pistil, **94,** 95
plant
    asexual reproduction in, 109, **109**
    characteristics of, 74–75
    classification of, 76–77, **77**
    evolution of, 27, 76, **76**
    fertilization in, 106, **106**
    gas exchange in, 112, **112**
    genetic engineering of, 42
    life cycle of, 75, **75**
    nonvascular, 76, **76, 77**
    organ systems of, 88–91

INDEX

reproduction in, 75, **75,** 106–109, **106–109**
responses to environment, 113–117, **113–117**
seasonal responses of, 115–117, **115–117**
seedless, 78–81, **78–81**
with seeds, 82–95, **82–95**
vascular, 76–77, **77**
plant disease, 32, **32,** 60, 62
plantlike protists, 48–51, **48–51**
Plasmodium vivax, 55, **55**
pneumonia, 32
poinsettia, 115, **115**
pollen, 82, 85, **85, 94,** 106, **106**
pollen tube, 106, **106**
pollination, 85–86, **85,** 106, **106**
by animals, 86, **86**
by insects, 86, **86**
by wind, 86, **86,** 95, **95**
pollution, bioremediation, 30, **30**
potato, 11, **11,** 48, 90, **109**
producers, 8, **8,** 27, 46
prokaryotes, 24
protein, 6, 10, **10**
amoebalike, 52–53, **52–53**
animal-like, 52–55, **52–55**
characteristics of, 46
plantlike, 48–51, **48–51**
protist, 46–56
reproduction of, 56, **56**
spore-forming, 55
Protista (kingdom), 46
protozoa, 52–55, **52–55**
with shells, 53, **53**
pseudopodia, 52, **52**
puffball, **58,** 62

R

radiolarians, 53, **53**
raffia palm, 92, **92**
red algae, 49
red blood cells, 11
red tide, 50, **50**
reproduction
as a characteristic of living things, 6, **6**
asexual, 6, **6,** 56, **56,** 58
in bacteria, 25, **25**
in fungi, 58
in plants, 75, **75,** 106–109
in protists, 56, **56**
sexual, 6, **6,** 56, **56,** 58
of viruses, 35, **35**
rhizoids, 78–79
rhizome, 80
root cap, 89, **89**
root hair, 89
roots, 88–89, **88–89**
functions of, 88
fungi growing on, 57
gravitropism of, 114, **114**
structure of, 89, **89**
types of, 89, **89**

rose, 82, 86–87
runner (plant), **109**
rusts, 62

S

sac fungi, 60, **60**
safety rules, 126–129
safety symbols, 126–129, **126–129**
salamanders, **8**
salt-loving bacteria, 28, **28**
scrambled egg slime mold, 47
seasons, causes of, 115, **115**
seaweed, 48–49, **48**
seed, 83, **83,** 95
development of, 107, **107**
dormant, 108
germination of, 83, 108, **108**
structure of, 83, **83**
seed coat, 83, **83**
seed plants, 82–91, **82–91**
seedless plants, 78–81, **78–81**
sepal, 94, **94**
sex cells, 75, **75**
sexual reproduction, 6, **6,** 56, **56,** 58
shell, of protozoa, 53, **53**
slime mold, **46–47,** 47
smuts, 62, **62**
soil, 79, 81
spider web, **10**
spirilla, 26
Spirogyra, 48
sporangia, **47,** 59, **59**
spore
of fungi, 58–61, **58–59**
plant, 75, **75**
of slime molds, 47, **47**
spore-forming protists, 55
sporophyte, 75, **75,** 82
sporozoan, **55**
spruce tree, 82, **84**
stamen, 94–95, **94**
starch, 11, **11**
detection with iodine, 11
stem, 90–91, **90**
bending toward light, 113, **113**
functions of, 90
gravitropism, 114, **114**
structure of, 91, **91**
underground, 90
stigma, **94–95,** 95, 106, **106**
stimulus, 5, **5**
stomata, 93, **93,** 112, **112**
strep throat, 32
sugar, 11, **11**
sweat, 5
symbiosis, 53, 57

T

taproot, 89, **89**
teeth, dental cavities, 32
threadlike fungi, 59

tobacco mosaic virus, 34
tomato, 91, **108**
transgenic plants, 42
transpiration, 112, **112**
tree rings, 91
tropism, 113–114, **113–114**
tuberculosis, 32
typhoid fever, 32

U

ulcer, 32

V

vaccine, 32, 42
variable, 145
vascular plants, 76–77, **77**
vein, leaf, 93, **93**
Venus' flytrap, **5**
viruses, 33–35, **33**
classification of, 34
diagnosis of bacterial diseases, 43
living or nonliving things, 33, **33**
lysogenic cycle of, 35, **35**
lytic cycle of, 35, **35**
pathogens, 33
shape of, 34
size of, 33
vitamins, 60
Volvox, 49, **49**

W

warbler, 9, **9**
water
as a necessity of life, 8
loss from leaf, 112, **112**
use in photosynthesis, 110–111, **111**
water mold, 48, **48**
wilting, 112
wood, 85, 91
woody stem, 91, **91**

X

xylem, 88, **89,** 90–91, **91**

Y

yeast, 60, **60**

Z

zooflagellates, **46**

Credits

Abbreviations used: (t) top, (c) center, (b) bottom, (l) left, (r) right, (bkgd) background

ILLUSTRATIONS

All illustrations, unless otherwise noted below by Holt, Rinehart and Winston.

Chapter One Page 7 (c), Will Nelson/Sweet Reps; 12 (b), Morgan-Cain & Associates; 12 (cl), Blake Thornton/Rita Marie; 13 (tr), David Merrell/Suzanne Craig Represents Inc.; 13 (cr), John White/The Neis Group; 13 (br), Morgan-Cain & Associates; 17 (cr), Blake Thornton/Rita Marie; 18 (bl), Morgan-Cain & Associates.

Chapter Two Page 25 (cl), Art and Science, Inc.; 26, Kip Carter; 29 (bl), Carlyn Iverson; 34 (cl), Morgan-Cain & Associates; 34 (c), Art and Science, Inc.; 34 (bl), Morgan-Cain & Associates; 34 (bc), Morgan-Cain & Associates; 41 (tr), Art and Science, Inc.

Chapter Three Page 51 (c), Scott Thorn Barrows/The Neis Group; 52 (c), Scott Thorn Barrows/The Neis Group; 54, Morgan-Cain & Associates; 55, Art and Science, Inc.; 58, Will Nelson/Sweet Reps.

Chapter Four Page 75 (tr), Morgan-Cain & Associates; 75 (bl), Sidney Jablonski; 77 (c), John White/The Neis Group; 78 (art), Ponde & Giles; 78 (arrows), Sidney Jablonski; 80 (art), Ponde & Giles; 80 (arrows), Sidney Jablonski; 83 (tr), Keith Locke; 83 (cl), Sarah Woods; 83 (br), James Gritz/Photonicia; 85 (art), Will Nelson/Sweet Reps; 85 (arrows), Sidney Jablonski; 87 (art), John White/The Neis Group; 87 (arrows), Sidney Jablonski; 88 (bl), Will Nelson/Sweet Reps; 89 (tr), John White/The Neis Group; 91 (r), Will Nelson/Sweet Reps; 93-94 (tr), Will Nelson/Sweet Reps; 98 (br), Sarah Woods; 101, Will Nelson/Sweet Reps.

Chapter Five Page106 (b), Will Nelson/Sweet Reps; 107 (c) Will Nelson/Sweet Reps; 108 (b), Will Nelson/Sweet Reps; 110 (c), Stephen Durke/Washington Artists; 111 (cl), Ponde & Giles; 112 (c), Morgan-Cain & Associates; 113 (bl), Carlyn Iverson; 115 (tr), Stephen Durke/Washington Artists; 115 (bl), Rob Schuster/Hankins and Tegenborg; 117 (c), Rob Schuster/Hankins and Tegenborg; 122 (cr), Will Nelson/Sweet Reps; 123 (cr), Carlyn Iverson.

LabBook Page 135 (br), 136 (br), Keith Locke.

Appendix Page 142 (t), Terry Guyer; 146 (b), Mark Mille/Sharon Langley; 800-801.

PHOTOGRAPHY

Cover and Title page: Visuals Unlimited/Robert W. Domm

Table of Contents: Page iv(t), CNRI/Science Photo Library/Photo Researchers, Inc.; iv(b), Robert Brons/BPS/Stone; v(t), David M. Phillips/Visuals Unlimited; v(c), Ken W. Davis/Tom Stack & Associates; v(b), Sam Dudgeon/HRW Photo; vi(t), Michael Fogden/DRK Photo; vi(c), Dwight R. Kuhn; vi(b), W. Cody/Westlight/Corbis; vii(t), David Phillips/Visuals Unlimited; vii(c), Dr. Norman R. Pace & Dr. Esther R. Angert; vii(b), Oliver Meckes/MPI-Tubingen/Photo Researchers, Inc.

Feature Borders: Unless otherwise noted below, all images copyright ©2001 PhotoDisc/HRW. "Across the Sciences" 71, all images by HRW; "Careers" 103, sand bkgd and Saturn, Corbis Images; DNA, Morgan Cain & Associates; scuba gear, ©1997 Radlund & Associates for Artville; "Eye on the Environment" 125, clouds and sea in bkgd, HRW; bkgd grass, red eyed frog, Corbis Images; hawks, pelican, Animals Animals/Earth Scenes; rat, Visuals Unlimited/John Grelach; endangered flower, Dan Suzio/Photo Researchers, Inc.; "Health Watch" 43, dumbbell, Sam Dudgeon/HRW Photo; aloe vera, EKG, Victoria Smith/HRW Photo; basketball, ©1997 Radlund & Associates for Artville; shoes, bubbles, Greg Geisler; "Scientific Debate" 20, Sam Dudgeon/HRW Photo; "Science Fiction" 21, saucers, Ian Christopher/Greg Geisler; book, HRW; bkgd telescope, Dave Cutler Studio, Inc./SIS; "Science Technology and Society" 42, 70, 102, robot, Greg Geisler; "Weird Science" 124, mite, David Burder/Stone; atom balls, J/B Woolsey Associates; walking stick, turtle, EclectiCollection.

Table of Contents: TK

Chapter One: pp. 2-3 Rick Friedman/Black Star Publishing/Picture Quest; 2 Dexter Sear/IO Vision; 3 HRW Photo; 4(tr), Visuals Unlimited/Cabisco; 4(bl), Visuals Unlimited/Science Visuals Unlimited; 4(br), Wolfgang Kaehler/Liaison International; 5(cl, cr), David M. Dennis/Tom Stack and Associates; 5(br), Visuals Unlimited/Fred Rohde; 6(tl), Visuals Unlimited/Stanley Flegler; 6(c), James M. McCann/Photo Researchers, Inc.; 6(bl), Lawrence Migdale/Photo Researchers, Inc.; 8 Robert Dunne/Photo Researchers, Inc.; 9(tr), Wolfgang Bayer; 9(cr), Visuals Unlimited/Rob Simpson; 10(bl), Photo Researchers, Inc.; 10(bc), Hans Reinhard/Bruce Coleman, Inc.; 16 Visuals Unlimited/Stanley Flegler; 17 Wolfgang Bayer; 19(bl), Dede Gilman/Unicorn Stock Photos; 20(tc, c), NASA.

Chapter Two: pp. 22-23 CAMR/A. B. Dowsett/Science Photo Library/Photo Researchers, Inc.; 23 HRW Photo; 24(c), Robert Yin/Corbis; 24(cr), Dr. Norman R. Pace and Dr. Esther R. Angert; 25(cr), Institut Pasteur/CNRI/Phototake; 25(bl),

Heather Angel; 26(bl), Visuals Unlimited/David M. Phillips; 26(cl), Fran Heyl Associates; 26(br), CNRI/Science Photo Library/Photo Researchers, Inc.; 27(tr), SuperStock; 27(b), Larry Ulrich/DRK Photo; 28 Richard T. Nowitz/ Corbis; 30(cr), Bio-Logic Remediation LTD; 30(tl), Sergio Purtell/FOCA; 32(tl), R. Sheridan/Ancient Art & Architecture Collection; 32(bl), Visuals Unlimited/Sherman Thomson; 33(b), E.O.S./Gelderblom/Photo Researchers, Inc.; 34(cl), Visuals Unlimited/Hans Gelderblom; 34(cr), Visuals Unlimited/K. G. Murti; 34(bl), Dr. O. Bradfute/Peter Arnold; 34(br), Oliver Meckes/MPI-Tubingen/Photo Researchers, Inc.; 38(b), Institut Pasteur/CNRI/Phototake; 38(c), Robert Yin/ Corbis; 38(cr), Dr. Norman R. Pace and Dr. Esther R. Angert; 40 Fran Heyl Associates; 42 HRW Photo composite; 43 Oliver Meckes/MPI-Tubingen/Photo Researchers, Inc.

Chapter Three: pp. 44-45 Steve Taylor/Stone; 45 HRW Photo; 46(tr), Visuals Unlimited/David Phillips; 46(bl), Matt Meadows/ Peter Arnold; 46(bc), Breck Kent; 46(c), Michael Abbey/Photo Researchers, Inc.; 47(cr), David M. Dennis/ Tom Stack; 47(b), Matt Meadows/Peter Arnold; 48(tl), Dr. Bruce Kendrick; 48(bl, br), Dr. E. R. Degginger; 49(cr), Kenneth W. Fink/Photo Researchers, Inc.; 49(br), Manfred Kage/Peter Arnold; 50(tl), Robert Brons/BPS/Stone; 50(b), Kevin Schafer/Peter Arnold; 52(bl) Parks/OSF/ Animals Animals; 53(tr), Manfred Kage/Peter Arnold; 53(br), George H. Harrison/Grant Heilman; 53(bc), Dr. Hossler/Custom Medical Stock Photo; 56(cl), Dr. Hilda Canter-Lund; 56(c), Eric Grave/Science Source/Photo Researchers, Inc.; 57(cr), Runk/Schoenberger/Grant Heilman; 57(cl), Visuals Unlimited/Stan Flegler; 57(bl), David M. Dennis/ Tom Stack; 57(c), R. Carr/Bruce Coleman; 58(bl) A. Davies/Bruce Coleman; 59(tr), Ralph Eague/Photo Researchers, Inc.; 59(b), Andrew Syred/Science Photo Library/Photo Researchers, Inc.; 60(tl), Gamma-Liaison; 60(c), J. Forsdyke/Gene Cox/Science Photo Library/Photo Researchers, Inc.; 60(bl), Laurie Campbell/NHPA; 61(tr), Visuals Unlimited/Wally Eberhart; 61(c, cl), Dr. E. R. Degginger; 62(tl), Michael Fogden/ DRK; 62(c), Visuals Unlimited/Inga Spence; 62(b), Walter H. Hodge/Peter Arnold; 63(c), John Gerlach/DRK Photo; 63(tr), Visuals Unlimited/Walt Anderson; 63(cr), Visuals Unlimited/Gerald & Buff Corsi; 66(cr) Visuals Unlimited/David Phillips; 67 David M. Dennis/Tom Stack; 68 David M. Dennis/ Tom Stack; 69(all), Omikron/Photo Researchers, Inc.; 70(all), Paul F. Hamlyn, BTTG; 71 Dr. James A. Pisarowicz/Wind Cave National Park.

Chapter Four: pp 72-73 Gary Braasch/CORBIS; 72 Wolfgand Kaehler/CORBIS; 73 HRW Photo; 74(cl), Robert Shafer/Stone; 74(bl, tr), SuperStock; 76(tc), Runk/Schoenberger/Grant Heilman; 76(bl), John Gerlach/Earth Scenes; 76(tl), Bruce Coleman, Inc.; 79(tr), Runk/Schoenberger/Grant Heilman; 79(bl), John Weinstein/The Field Museum, Chicago, IL; 80(tl), Larry Ulrich/DRK Photo; 80(c), SuperStock; 81(tr), Ed Reschke/Peter Arnold; 81(cr), Runk/Schoenberger/Grant Heilman; 82(tr), Robert Barclay/Grant Heilman; 82(cl), Heather Angel; 82(br), Phil Degginger; 84(tl), Tom Bean; 84(tc), Jim Strawser/Grant Heilman; 84(br), Visuals Unlimited/John D. Cunningham; 84(bl), Walter H. Hodge/Peter Arnold; 85(tr) Patti Murray/Earth Scenes; 86(tl), William E. Ferguson; 86(bl), Werner H. Muller/Peter Arnold; 86(bc), Grant Heilman; 86(br), SuperStock; 89(bc), Runk/Schoenberger/ Grant Heilman; 89(bc), Nigel Cattlin/Holt Studios International/Photo Researchers, Inc.; 89(bl), Dwight R. Kuhn; 89(tr), Ed Reschke/Peter Arnold, Inc.; 89(cr), Runk/Rannels/Grant Heilman Photography; 90(tc), Harry Smith Collection; 90(cl), Larry Ulrich/DRK Photo; 90(bc), Michael Abbey/Peter Arnold; 90(br), Dale E. Boyer/Photo Researchers, Inc.; 91(tl), Stephen J. Krasemann/Photo Researchers, Inc.; 91(tr), Tom Bean; 92(tr), Index Stock Photography; 92(tl, bc), Dr. E.R. Degginger; 92(cl), Gary B. Braasch; 93(br) Ken W. Davis/Tom Stack; 94(tl), SuperStock; 95(tr), George Bernard/ Science Photo Library/Photo Researchers, Inc.; 95(c), Patrick Jones/Corbis; 98(c) The Field Museum, Chicago, IL; 99 SuperStock; 100(br) Kevin Adams/ Liaison International; 102 Carl Redmond/University of Kentucky; 103(tl), Mark Philbrick/Brigham Young University; 103(br), Phillip-Lorca DiCorcia.

Chapter Five: pp. 104-105 Breck P. Kent/Animals Animals; 105 HRW Photo; 108(tl), Visuals Unlimited/W. Ormerod; 108(tc), George Bernard/Earth Scenes; 108(tr), Image Copyright ©2001 Photodisc, Inc.; 109(tr), Paul Hein/Unicorn; 109(cr), Jerome Wexler/Photo Researchers, Inc.; 109(cl), George Bernard/Earth Scenes; 110(br), Gregg Hadel/Stone; 112(tl), Dr. Jeremy Burgess/Science Photo Library/Photo Researchers, Inc.; 113(br), Cathlyn Melloan/Stone; 114(cl, cr), R. F. Evert; 115(c), Dick Keen/Unicorn; 115(b), Visuals Unlimited/E. Webber; 116(tr), W. Cody/WestLight; 116(bl, bc, br), Rich Iwasaki/Stone; 117(tl), Visuals Unlimited/ Bill Beatty; 117(cl), Visuals Unlimited/Bill Beatty; 121(cl) R. F. Evert; 121(tr, cr, br), Rich Iwasaki/Stone; 123(b), W. Cody/Westlight; 124(cl), Discover Syndication/Walt Disney Publications; 124(bc), David Littschwager & Susan Middleton/Discover Magazine; 124(br), Discover Syndication/Walt Disney Publications; 125(cr), Cary S. Wolinsky.

Labook: "LabBook Header": "L", Corbis Images, "a", Letraset-Phototone, "b" and "B", HRW, "o" and "k", Images Copyright ©2001 PhotoDisc, Inc.; 118-119, Sam Dudgeon/HRW Photo; 127(cl), Michelle Bridwell/HRW Photo; 127(br), Image Copyright ©2001 Photodisc, Inc.; 128(cl) Victoria Smith/HRW Photo; 128(bl), Stephanie Morris/HRW Photo; 129(tr), Jana Birchum/HRW Photo; 137(bc), Breck P. Kent; 137(br), Stephen J. Krasemann/ Photo Researchers, Inc.; 137(c), Visuals Unlimited/R. Calentine; 137(t), Runk/ Schoenberger/Grant Heilman.

Appendix: p. 158 CENCO

Sam Dudgeon/HRW Photos: all Systems of the Body background photos, viii-1, 10(br), 11, 14, 19(tr, cr, br), 110(bl), 126, 127(b); 128(tr, br), 129(tl), 130, 131, 133, 135, 138, 143(br).

Peter Van Steen/HRW Photos: p. 15, 31(tr, bl), 36, 41, 65, 129(b), 143(tr).

John Langford/HRW Photos: p. 127(tr).

Acknowledgements continued from page iii.

Alyson Mike
Science Teacher
East Valley Middle School
East Helena, Montana

Donna Norwood
Science Teacher and Dept. Chair
Monroe Middle School
Charlotte, North Carolina

James B. Pulley
Former Science Teacher
Liberty High School
Liberty, Missouri

Terry J. Rakes
Science Teacher
Elmwood Junior High School
Rogers, Arkansas

Elizabeth Rustad
Science Teacher
Crane Middle School
Yuma, Arizona

Debra A. Sampson
Science Teacher
Booker T. Washington Middle School
Elgin, Texas

Charles Schindler
Curriculum Advisor
San Bernadino City Unified Schools
San Bernadino, California

Bert J. Sherwood
Science Teacher
Socorro Middle School
El Paso, Texas

Patricia McFarlane Soto
Science Teacher and Dept. Chair
G. W. Carver Middle School
Miami, Florida

David M. Sparks
Science Teacher
Redwater Junior High School
Redwater, Texas

Elizabeth Truax
Science Teacher
Lewiston-Porter Central School
Lewiston, New York

Ivora Washington
Science Teacher and Dept. Chair
Hyattsville Middle School
Washington, D.C.

Elsie N. Waynes
Science Teacher and Dept. Chair
R. H. Terrell Junior High School
Washington, D.C.

Nancy Wesorick
Science and Math Teacher
Sunset Middle School
Longmont, Colorado

Alexis S. Wright
Middle School Science Coordinator
Rye Country Day School
Rye, New York

John Zambo
Science Teacher
E. Ustach Middle School
Modesto, California

Gordon Zibelman
Science Teacher
Drexell Hill Middle School
Drexell Hill, Pennsylvania

Self-Check Answers

Chapter 1—It's Alive!! Or, Is It?

Page 5: Your alarm clock is a stimulus. It rings, and you respond by shutting it off and getting out of bed.

Chapter 2—Bacteria and Viruses

Page 27: Cyanobacteria were once classified as plants because they use photosynthesis to make food.

Chapter 3—Protists and Fungi

Page 48: No, some funguslike protists are parasites or consumers.

Page 54: 1. Cilia are used to move a ciliate through the water and to sweep food toward the organism. 2. Ciliates are classified as animal-like protists because they are consumers and they move.

Page 58: 1. Both are consumers that secrete digestive juices onto a food source and then absorb the digested nutrients. Both reproduce asexually by spores. 2. Hyphae grow together to form the mycelium.

Page 59: Spores are contained in sporangia.

Chapter 4—Introduction to Plants

Page 76: Plants need a cuticle to keep the leaves from drying out. Algae grow in a wet environment, so they do not need a cuticle.

Page 92: Stems hold up the leaves so that the leaves can get adequate sunshine for photosynthesis.

Chapter 5—Plant Processes

Page 107: Fruit develops from the ovary, so the flower can have only one fruit. Seeds develop from the ovules, so there should be six seeds.

Page 111: The sun is the source of the energy in sugar.

Page 114: 1. (See concept map below.)
2. During negative phototropism, the plant would grow away from the stimulus (light), so it would be bending to the left.

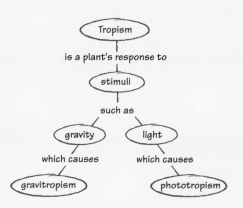